GCSE

Design & Technology Graphic Products

Complete Revision and Practice

Contents

Contents

Published by Coordination Group Publications Ltd.

Editors:
Keri Barrow, Ellen Bowness, Dominic Hall, Kate Houghton, Simon Little, Rachel Selway.

Contributors:
Juliet Cash, Martin Chester, Stephen Guinness, Gemma Hallam, Kerry Kolbe, Tim Major, Alan Nanson, Andy Park, Karen Steel, Claire Thompson, Philip Thompson, Julie Wakeling, Steve Whittle and Anthony Wilcock.

With thanks to Ed Robinson and Lucy Workman for the proofreading.

AQA material is reproduced by kind permission of the Assessment and Qualifications Alliance.

OCR examination questions are reproduced by kind permission of OCR.

ISBN: 978 1 84146 389 6
Website: www.cgpbooks.co.uk
Printed by Elanders Hindson Ltd, Newcastle upon Tyne.
Clipart from CorelDRAW®
With thanks to TECHSOFT UK LTD for permission to use a screenshot from Techsoft Design Tools — 2D Design.
Also with thanks to PTC for permission to use a screenshot from Pro/DESKTOP™. Pro/DESKTOP™ is a Windows native parametric feature based solid modeller developed by PTC.
Image of PONGO® Smiley reproduced with kind permission of David Franklin Ltd.

Design Brief

The process of <u>designing</u> and <u>making</u> something is called 'the design process'. The whole process can take a while — so it's usually broken down into smaller <u>chunks</u>.

The **design process** is similar in **industry** and **school**

It's no accident that the things you'll have to do for your <u>Design and Technology project</u> are pretty similar to what happens in <u>industry</u>.

- The best products are those that address a <u>real need</u>.
- That's why companies spend so much <u>time</u> and <u>money</u> on <u>customer research</u>. The more people there are who would actually <u>use</u> a product, the more chance it stands of being a <u>roaring success</u>.
- The <u>best</u> ideas for Design and Technology <u>projects</u> are also those that meet a genuine need.

The rest of this section describes a <u>typical design process</u>. It shows the sort of thing that happens in <u>industry</u> every day. It also shows the stages you need to go through while you're putting a <u>Design and Technology project</u> together.

First get your **idea** for a **new product**

Whether you're working in the research and development department of a multinational company, or you're putting together your project, you need to explain <u>why</u> a new product is <u>needed</u>. It could be for one of the following reasons:

1) There are <u>problems</u> with an existing product.
2) The <u>performance</u> of an existing design could be <u>improved</u>.
3) There's a <u>gap</u> in the market that you want to fill.

The **design brief** explains **why** your product is **needed**

The <u>design brief</u> explains <u>why</u> there might be a need for a new product. It should include the following:

1) An <u>outline</u> of the <u>problem</u> and who it <u>affects</u>.
2) The <u>need</u> arising from the problem.
3) What you <u>intend</u> to do about it (e.g. design and make...).
4) How your product will be <u>used</u>.
5) The <u>environment</u> it will be used in.

Basically, the design brief should concentrate on the <u>problem</u> you're trying to <u>solve</u>.

Your design brief should start by describing the problem

Your design brief should be simple and concise. A design brief should <u>not</u> be a detailed description of what you intend to make — you can only say this after you've designed it and tried things out. <u>Describe the problem</u> first. The rest comes later.

Research

Once you've written your design brief, you can start researching your project.

Research can help you get *ideas*

It's worth doing your research carefully — it can give you loads of ideas for the rest of the design process. The point of doing research is to:

1) Check that people will actually want your product (although you might have done this already when you chose your project).
2) Find out what makes an existing product good or bad — talk to people who actually use this kind of product, and see what they like or dislike.
3) Find out the materials, pre-manufactured components and techniques you can use, and how they will affect the manufacturing and selling costs.
4) Give you a good starting point for designing.

There are different *kinds* of research

You can do different kinds of research. This might include:

(1) Questionnaires — to find out people's likes/dislikes and so on. This will help you identify your target group and find out market trends (e.g. what things are becoming more popular).

(2) Disassembling a product (i.e. taking it apart) — this will help you find out how a current product is made and how it works. It could also give you information about different materials and processes used, and how existing products meet potential users' needs.

(3) Measuring — to find out the weights and sizes of current products. This might give you an idea of the possible size, shape and weight of your product. You could also do some kind of sensory analysis (e.g. you could see how it feels and looks).

Research analysis means drawing *conclusions*

Once you've done your research, you'll need to come to some conclusions. This means deciding how to use the information to help you with your design. This is called research analysis.

Try to do the following:

1) Pick out the useful information.
2) Explain what impact the research will have on your designs.
3) Suggest ways forward from the research gathered.

By the time you've done all this, you should have some ideas about how to tackle your project.

You can never have too many ideas

Research is important. You could spend some time doing 'book research', e.g. finding out about any British or European standards your product will have to meet. The internet is also a useful research tool.

Design Specification

Once you've picked out the main points of your research, you're ready to put together a design specification.

The **design specification** is a **list** of **conditions to meet**

The design specification describes the restrictions and possibilities of the product. It's a good point to start from when you get round to doing the more creative stuff.

1) The design specification gives certain conditions that the product will have to meet. Try to put your specification together in bullet form as specific points, rather than a paragraph of explanations.

> E.g. if your research tells you that people would never buy an MP3 player that was longer than 12cm, then your design specification might include the statement, "Must be less than 12cm in length."

2) You should include some or all of the following:
- a description of how it should look
- details about what it has to do/be
- materials, ingredients and joining methods
- details of size/weight
- safety points to consider
- financial constraints

Compare your designs with the **design specification**

1) Once you've come up with a design, you need to compare it to the specification and confirm that each point is satisfied.

> E.g. If your design specification contains these two points, then all of your designs should be less than 120 mm long and have a metal case.

> "The maximum length will be 120 mm."
> "The product should have a metal case."

2) Some points might be harder to compare to your specification simply by looking at the product.

> E.g. "The product should feel comfortable."

For this, you'll need to get someone to test the product once it's been made/modelled.

You might need to make **more than one** specification

You'll probably need to produce several specifications as your project develops:

> Initial Design Specification — this is your first design specification. It should be done after your research analysis.

1) As you develop your design, you'll probably want to make some changes to your design specification. This is fine, as long as your design brief is being met and you have taken your research analysis into account.

2) Maybe as a result of some of your modelling (see page 10) you'll find that certain materials aren't suitable. You can add this information to an updated specification.

3) You can keep doing this until you end up with a final product specification.

The design specification is where you use your research

Making a design specification is a vital step in designing and manufacturing a new product. So learn about it.

Generating Proposals

This is where it all starts to get a bit more <u>interesting</u>. This is the <u>creative</u> bit, where you start <u>generating ideas</u>.

There are a few **tricks** that can help you **get started**

The following are suggestions to help you get started with designing:

1) Create a <u>mood board</u> — this is a load of different images, words, materials, colours and so on that might trigger ideas for your design.

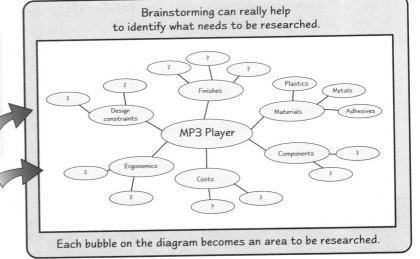

Brainstorming can really help to identify what needs to be researched.

2) <u>Brainstorm</u> — think up key words, questions and initial thoughts relating to your product. (Start off by just writing whatever ideas come into your head — analyse them later.)

This is sometimes called a spider diagram.

Each bubble on the diagram becomes an area to be researched.

3) Work from an <u>existing product</u> — but change some of its features or production methods so that it fits in with your <u>specification</u>.

4) Break the task up into smaller parts — e.g. design the 'look' of the product (<u>aesthetics</u>), then look at the <u>technology</u> involved and so on.

Mood boards and brainstorming help to generate ideas
When you're making spider diagrams write down everything that comes into your head. If you find something (e.g. a photo, a bit of card / plastic) you think might be useful for your design, stick it on your mood board.

Generating Proposals

You'll need lots of ideas to come up with brilliant designs.

You need to come up with a *range of designs*

1) You need to <u>annotate</u> (i.e. add <u>notes</u> to) your designs to fully <u>explain</u> your ideas. These notes could be about:

- materials
- size
- users
- shape
- cost
- advantages and disadvantages
- production method
- functions

They might look something like this:

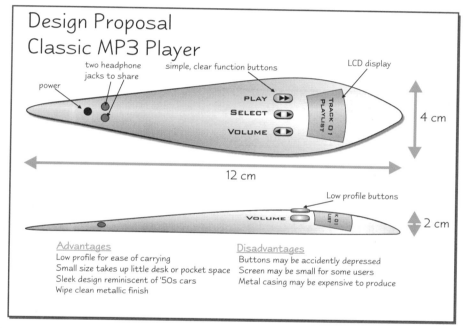

Design Proposal
Classic MP3 Player

power
two headphone jacks to share
simple, clear function buttons
LCD display

PLAY ▶▶
SELECT ◀▶
VOLUME ◀▶
TRACK 01 PLAYLIST

4 cm

12 cm

Low profile buttons
VOLUME
2 cm

<u>Advantages</u>
Low profile for ease of carrying
Small size takes up little desk or pocket space
Sleek design reminiscent of '50s cars
Wipe clean metallic finish

<u>Disadvantages</u>
Buttons may be accidently depressed
Screen may be small for some users
Metal casing may be expensive to produce

2) You need to produce a <u>wide range</u> of <u>appropriate solutions</u> that you think could <u>actually be made</u>.

3) Try to use a <u>range of techniques</u> for presenting your designs. A good thing to do is to use different drawing techniques — for example:

- perspective
- orthographic projection
- cross-sections
- freehand sketching
- digital camera photos
- isometric projection

4) Once you've got a few possible designs, you need to <u>check</u> that each one <u>matches</u> your <u>specification</u> — any that don't will <u>not</u> be <u>suitable</u>.

5) Finally, you need to choose <u>one</u> of your suitable designs to <u>develop further</u>.

Remember — all your ideas have to match your specification

Think about what someone will need to know to fully appreciate your design, and include this information on your proposal. And remember — you need to do quite a few of these so that you can choose the best one to develop and improve. This is the time to get creative.

Development

Once you've decided on a design, you can begin to develop it further.
This is when your design should start to really take shape.

You can develop your design in different ways

Depending on the type of product that's being produced, further development might involve:

1) Producing further sketches — but in more detail, e.g. recording the sizes
   of fittings and components, and dimensions for component positions.
   Also sketching how parts should be constructed and fitted together.
2) Modelling your idea. This lets you test that it works and also allows you to experiment
   with different aspects of the design. E.g. you could try various materials, sizes and
   production methods.
3) Using people's opinions about developments to help you arrive at a satisfactory solution.

Modelling means trying things out

It can be useful to prototype or model your idea, especially if it's difficult to draw.

1) Try out different aspects of your design. If your design is quite complex it may help
   to break it down into smaller, more manageable parts and test them individually.
2) Use a camera (digital or otherwise) to record your models.
3) Evaluate the models (see next page), identifying reasons for selecting or rejecting
   different designs.

> This is a vital part of the design process. Ideally you should
> solve all the potential problems with your design at this stage.

Use the results to make modifications

1) Results from your modelling and from your evaluation (see next page) will help you make important
   modifications (changes) to improve the product, and help it meet the design specification.
2) Suggested improvements could be:
   - ways to make the product itself better,
   - suggestions to make it more suitable for mass production (see page 97).
3) But make sure you keep a record of whatever it is you find out (see next page).
4) Once you've made a modification to your design, you'll need to try it out to see if it actually
   improves things.
5) You might find that you end up modifying something, then trying it out, then making another
   modification and trying that out, then making another modification and trying that out, and so on.

Modelling is more useful than you'd think

Modelling and evaluation (see next page) go hand in hand. It's pointless building a model
and trying it out if you're not going to bother learning anything from it. So keep thinking
about and evaluating your work at all times.

Evaluation

Evaluation is an important part of any product development process.
It needs to be done at various stages along the way.

Keep **records** of your **research** and **testing**

1) As you develop your product, keep records of any testing or market research you do. Write it all down, keep it, and refer back to it.

2) You might have tested materials for suitability, or tested components to see how well they work — but whatever you did, you need to write down all the results.

3) Compare the good and bad points of existing products with your model or prototype. Ask yourself if your product does the job better. Record your results.

4) Find out people's opinions and preferences about your models and prototypes (see previous page). This will help you to refine your ideas so you can arrive at the best solution.

5) Questionnaires help here — relevant market research questions might include:

- Does the product work well?
- Does the product work as well as similar products on the market?
- Does the product look good? Is it well styled and modern-looking?
- Are you unsure about any of the features? If so, which ones and why?
- If this product were on the market, would you consider buying it?
- If you were buying it, which price range do you think it would fall into?
- Do you prefer another similar product to this one?

> This type of evaluation is called formative evaluation — because it's being used to help form the final design.

You should know **exactly** what you're making

By the time you've finished developing your ideas and have arrived at a final design, you should have found out / worked out:

1) The best materials, tools and other equipment to use (and their availability). This might include identifying any pre-manufactured components you're going to use.

2) The approximate manufacturing time needed to make each item.

3) How much it should cost to manufacture each item.

4) The most appropriate assembly process — this is going to be important information when it comes to planning production, and can be in the form of a flow chart (see page 13).

If you don't know what you're doing now, you never will...

At this stage of the process it should be crystal clear in your own mind how your final product should look, and how you're going to make it. But you're not finished yet. There's still the little business of actually making your pride and joy.

Manufacturer's Specification

Now that you know <u>exactly</u> what you're going to make, you need to <u>communicate</u> all that information to the person who's actually going to <u>make</u> it.

You need to produce a *manufacturer's specification*

A manufacturer's specification can be a written <u>series of statements</u>, or <u>working drawings</u> and <u>sequence diagrams</u>. It has to explain <u>exactly</u> how the product will be made, and should include:

1) Clear <u>construction</u> details explaining <u>exactly</u> how each bit's going to be made.

2) <u>Sizes</u> — <u>precise measurements</u> of each part.

3) <u>Tolerances</u> — the maximum and minimum sizes each part should be.

4) <u>Finishing</u> details — any special sequences for finishing.

5) <u>Quality control</u> instructions — where, when and how the manufacturing process and product quality should be checked. (See page 13 for time planning and page 72 for quality control).

6) <u>Costings</u> — how much each part costs, and details of any other costs involved.

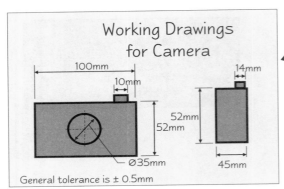

<u>Working drawings</u> give the precise <u>dimensions</u> of the product.

<u>Spreadsheets</u> are great for working out <u>costings</u>.

Plan how long the *production process* should take

When you get to this stage of product development, you also need to plan:

1) How your methods might have to <u>change</u> to manufacture the product <u>in volume</u>.

2) <u>Each stage</u> of the process in a great deal of <u>detail</u>.

3) <u>How long</u> each stage will take.

4) What needs to be <u>prepared</u> before you can start each stage.

5) How you will <u>ensure consistency</u> and <u>quality</u>.

See the next page as well for some different ways to help with this planning.

The devil's in the detail

This part of the design process is about detail and precision. Your manufacturer's specification has to be spot on, or you end up wasting a lot of time and wasting materials.

Planning Production

Making one or two examples of your product is (relatively) easy. But mass-producing it is a whole different ball game. And it takes a lot of careful planning.

Use *charts* to help you

You need to work out <u>how long</u> each stage will take, and how these times will fit into the <u>total time</u> you've allowed for production. There are different ways of doing this:

1) <u>Work Order</u>

This can be produced as a <u>table</u> or <u>flow chart</u>. The purpose of a work order is to plan <u>in sequence</u> each task to be carried out. This will also include: tools and equipment, quality control stages, safety, and so on.

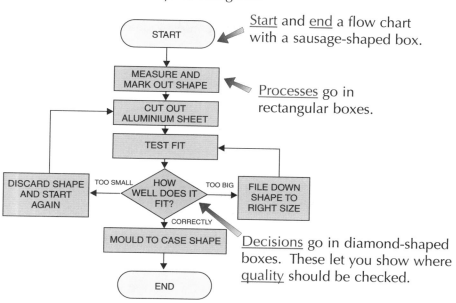

<u>Start</u> and <u>end</u> a flow chart with a sausage-shaped box.

<u>Processes</u> go in rectangular boxes.

<u>Decisions</u> go in diamond-shaped boxes. These let you show where <u>quality</u> should be checked.

2) <u>Gantt Chart</u>

This is a time plan showing the <u>management</u> of tasks. The tasks are listed down the <u>left-hand</u> side, and the <u>timing</u> plotted across the top. The coloured squares show <u>how long</u> each task takes, and the <u>order</u> they're done in.

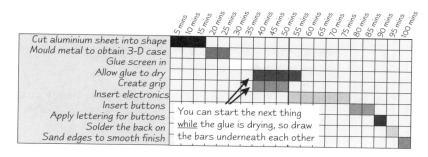

Test that the product *works* and meets the *specification*

1) When you think you've got the final product, it's vital to <u>test</u> it. Most important of all, you have to make sure it <u>works</u>, and meets the original <u>design specification</u>.

2) More <u>questionnaires</u> or <u>surveys</u> may help here. Ask a wide range of people to give their opinions about the finished product.

3) If your product <u>fails</u> to match any part of the <u>specification</u>, you must explain <u>why</u>. You really have to stand back and have a good hard think about your work. If you aren't satisfied with the way any part of the process went, think of how you could put it right for next time. Write it down in the form of a <u>report</u>.

4) This type of final evaluation is called <u>summative evaluation</u> — it summarises what you've learnt.

Proper planning is a big time saver

So, that's all you have to do when it comes to your project.
In a few short weeks you can achieve what people in industry take several months to do.

Warm-up and Worked Exam Questions

These warm-up questions should ease you gently in and make sure you've got the basics straight. If there's anything you've forgotten, check up on the facts before you do the exam questions.

Warm-up Questions

1) In the design process, which comes first, the brief or the specification?
2) Name two different types of research that could be part of the design process.
3) Name two different design considerations when re-designing a clock.
4) In the design process, what is design development for?
5) In a Work Order Diagram, what does this shape box mean?
6) Name the two types of information that a Gantt Chart connects together.

Exam questions are the best way to practise what you've learnt — they're exactly what you'll have to do on the big day. Read carefully through this worked example, then try the questions on the next page.

Worked Exam Questions

1   Terri is a graphic designer, and has been asked by the Topps Chocolate Company to re-design some of their Easter egg packaging.

   a)   Explain why Terri needs to know the age group of intended customers for the chocolate egg box?

   So the design of the art work is appropriate for the target age group.

   Here 'appropriate' means 'suitable for the age range of the intended users'.
   (1 mark)

   b)   Describe two suitable design attributes of an Easter egg package, designed specifically for children under the age of nine.

   The colour scheme should be bright and cheerful. Also the artwork could have a popular cartoon figure on it.
   (2 marks)

2   Terri carried out a survey of potential customers' preferences. The results showed that they preferred a package shape in the form of a cartoon character.

   a)   How should this information influence Terri's on-going research?

   She should do more detailed research on cartoon characters.
   (1 mark)

   b)   Suggest what she could do for her follow up research.

   She could find out which cartoons are children's favourites, how to get copyright to use the cartoon characters and how much this would cost.
   (2 marks)

3   Bruce is a graphic designer working on the packaging for a new mobile phone. The brief given to Bruce was 'design some new packaging'. Explain why this brief is problematic for both Bruce and the client.

....

....

(2 marks)

4   Before starting any designs, Bruce has decided to research the chosen market by using a questionnaire/survey. He wants to find out about the design preferences of 250 teenagers.

   a)   Suggest two suitable closed questions Bruce could ask.

....

....

(2 marks)

   b)   i)   Explain the purpose of Bruce's survey.

....

(1 mark)

      ii)   Explain the purpose of the design specification.

....

(1 mark)

      iii)   Explain the connection between the design specification and the survey.

....

....

(2 marks)

5   Bruce made a presentation to the client showing a set of early ideas. The client made it clear that they had a strong preference for one of the designs.

   a)   Why should Bruce now develop this design idea to produce several variations?

....

(1 mark)

   b)   Suggest three different ways that Bruce could develop his design ideas.

....

....

....

(3 marks)

Exam Questions

6   To communicate his ideas effectively, Bruce has produced a packaging prototype model.

    a)   List three things that Bruce could do to evaluate the model.

....

....

(3 marks)

    b)   List three advantages Bruce would gain by evaluating the model at this stage in the design process.

....

....

....

(3 marks)

7   When Bruce had completed his final design, he produced a manufacturer's specification.

    a)   Explain what the manufacturer's specification is.

....

....

....

(3 marks)

    b)   State three things that Bruce might include in his manufacturer's specification.

....

....

....

(3 marks)

Revision Summary for Section One

Try the revision questions, and then have a look back through the section to see if you got them all right. If you did — great. But if you got any wrong, have another careful read of the section and then <u>try the questions again</u>. And keep doing this until you can get all the questions right. That way, you know you're learning...

1)   What is the name given to the whole process of designing and making something?

2)   Give three reasons why a new product might be needed.

3)   Describe the kind of information you should put in your design brief.

4)   Give three ways in which research can help you when you're designing a new product.

5)   Explain how a questionnaire can be useful when designing or researching a product.

6)   Give two other methods you could use to carry out research.

7)   What is the name given to the process of drawing conclusions from your research?

8)   Explain what is meant by a design specification.

9)   Why might some points in a design specification be hard to assess just by looking at the product?

10) When would you compile an initial design specification?

11) Give three ways of generating ideas.

12) What does the word 'annotate' mean?

13) What information should you include in your designs?

14) Why should you aim to produce a number of design ideas?

15) Give three techniques for presenting your designs.

16) Name two ways of developing your designs further.

17) Explain why it's useful to model your designs.

18) Describe two kinds of improvement you could make to your design.

19) When should you make an evaluation of your design? a) at the end of the project
     b) throughout the project   c) at the start of the project.

20) Describe two ways of evaluating your work.

21) What is meant by the phrase 'formative evaluation'?

22) Explain why a manufacturer's specification needs to be very precise.

23) Give four kinds of information that need to be on a manufacturer's specification.

24) When using a Gantt chart, what information goes down the left-hand side?

25) Describe two methods of planning how long the manufacturing process should take.

26) What is a 'summative evaluation'?

Paper

There are loads of different types of <u>paper</u> — each designed to suit a particular situation.

There are loads of types of paper you need to **know about** and **use**

1) <u>Cartridge paper</u> has a <u>textured</u> surface, which is great for sketching with pencils, crayons, pastels, gouache, inks and watercolours.

2) <u>Layout paper</u> is <u>thin</u> and <u>translucent</u> (you can see light through it) and is used for general design work — particularly generating ideas.

3) <u>Bleed-proof paper</u> is used by designers when drawing with <u>felt-tips</u> and <u>marker pens</u>. The ink doesn't spread out (<u>bleed</u>) — it stays put.

4) <u>Tracing paper</u> is <u>translucent</u>, and is used to <u>copy images</u>.

5) <u>Photocopy paper</u> is probably the paper you use most in <u>class</u>. It's most commonly used in either <u>A4</u> or <u>A3</u> sizes. It's <u>cheap</u>.

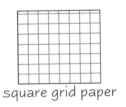

square grid paper

6) <u>Grid paper</u> may have a <u>square</u>, <u>isometric</u> or <u>perspective</u> pre-printed pattern on it — <u>square grid paper</u> is useful for orthographic drawings and <u>nets</u> (for product developments), and <u>isometric grid paper</u> is good for <u>presentation drawings</u>.

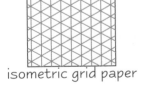

isometric grid paper

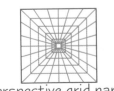

perspective grid paper

Make a table of the different papers and their uses

Knowing all the different types of paper can really help when it comes to designing your project. You'll be able to pick the right paper for the task that you're doing.

Board

There are also loads of different types of <u>board</u>:

You need to **know** about **six kinds** of **board**

The weight of paper and card is measured in <u>gsm</u> (grams per square metre).

Above 200 gsm, it's not paper any more — it's <u>board</u>.

1) <u>Mounting card</u> is used to mount drawings and photographs for presentation or framing — usually by cutting a 'window'.

2) <u>Foamboard</u> (polystyrene foam laminated between card) is lightweight and is used for models and mounting.

3) <u>Solid white board</u> has a high quality bleached surface, which is ideal for printing, and is used loads in primary packaging, i.e. the packaging that's used for individual items (as opposed to secondary packaging, which might be a big box used to transport lots of the same item to shops, etc.).

4) <u>Corrugated card</u> is used a lot in <u>secondary</u> packaging to protect products during transit. It's made up of a <u>fluted inner core</u> sandwiched between <u>two outer layers</u>.

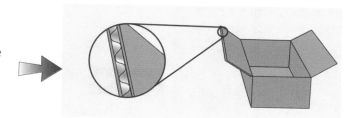

5) <u>Duplex board</u> has a <u>different colour</u> and <u>texture</u> on <u>each side</u>. It's often used where only <u>one surface</u> is <u>seen</u>, so that only one side needs to be <u>smooth</u> for <u>printing</u>. It's <u>unbleached</u>, so it's ideal for <u>food packaging</u>.

6) <u>Klett</u> is a type of <u>corrugated board</u> used in packaging which uses <u>double-sided tape</u> instead of <u>cow gum</u> to bond it together.

Board is often made from **recycled paper**

1) As paper and card are made from wood pulp, most of it's <u>recyclable</u> and from <u>sustainable resources</u>.

2) It's therefore <u>environmentally friendly</u>.

3) A lot of <u>cardboard</u> is made from recycled material:

<u>Sustainable resources</u> are resources like trees that can be <u>renewed</u>, so they will never run out.
<u>Non-sustainable resources</u> will eventually <u>run out</u>. These are things like oil, which is used to make plastic.

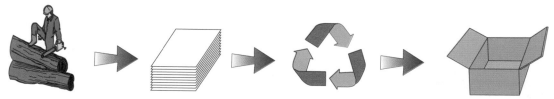

Heavier than 200 gsm means it's board

There are a few things to remember on this page — names of boards, their characteristics and what they are usually used for. Bet you didn't know there were so many different types of board...

Plastics — Types and Uses

Plastics (polymers and copolymers) are <u>synthetic resinous substances</u> that can be <u>moulded</u> with the aid of heat and/or pressure.

There are **two** main **classes** of plastics

① <u>Thermosetting</u> plastics — ones that once moulded cannot be remoulded.

② <u>Thermoplastics</u> — ones that are moulded by heating and, if heated again, can be remoulded.

Thermoplastics are used for loads of things

ACETATE (Cellulose acetate)

Acetate is <u>hard</u>, <u>shiny</u> and <u>transparent/translucent</u>. It's used in badge-making, for overhead projector transparencies and packaging.

acetate

ACRYLIC

acrylic

Acrylic, e.g. <u>polymethyl methacrylate</u> is also known as <u>perspex</u> or <u>plexiglas</u>. Acrylics are <u>hard</u>, <u>shiny</u> and <u>brittle</u>. They're used in schools a lot and come in loads of different colours. They can be used to make menu holders (for example), using a <u>line-bender</u> (see p22), and can also be used to make baths, signs, etc. Acrylics are also used in the paint and textile industries.

POLYETHYLENE (Polythene)

Polythene comes in two main types. <u>Low-density polyethylene</u> (<u>LDPE</u>) is <u>soft</u> and <u>flexible</u> — it's used for packaging, carrier bags, washing-up liquid bottles, etc. <u>High-density polyethylene</u> (<u>HDPE</u>) is <u>stiff</u> and <u>strong</u>, and is used for things like washing-up bowls.

polythene

POLYESTERS

polyester

Polyesters (e.g. polyethylene terephthalate — <u>PET</u>) have a variety of uses, e.g. drink bottles and clothing.

POLYPROPYLENE (PP)

Polypropylene is <u>tough</u> and <u>flexible</u>. Products can be made with a 'living hinge' (box, lid and hinge all made out of one piece of polypropylene) — which is handy for lunch boxes, etc. It's also used for many different kinds of packaging, chairs, textiles and automotive components.

polypropylene

Plastics — Types and Uses

Here are some more examples of thermoplastics...

POLYSTYRENE (PS)

Polystyrene comes in two main types. <u>Expanded PS</u> (<u>STYROFOAM</u>™) is <u>white</u>, <u>lightweight</u> and <u>crumbly</u>. It is used in <u>protective</u> packaging, <u>insulating</u> packaging and for filling beanbags. It can be shaped easily with a <u>hot-wire cutter</u> to produce accurate 3-D mock-ups and models. <u>Rigid/high impact PS</u> comes in a variety of colours and thicknesses and is used for <u>vacuum forming</u> and <u>fabricating</u> boxes for products.

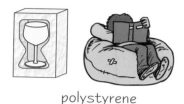

polystyrene

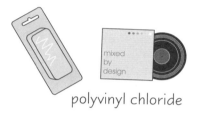

polyvinyl chloride

POLYVINYL CHLORIDE (PVC)

PVC is quite brittle (snaps easily). It's used for <u>blister packs</u>, window frames, <u>vinyl records</u> and interesting clothes.

Mylar®

<u>Mylar</u>® is a type of polyester film used for <u>stencils</u>.

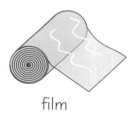

film

LOW-TACK MASKING FILM

<u>Low-tack masking film</u> is used to position sticky-backed vinyl (cut with computer numerically controlled <u>STIKA</u> or <u>CAMM</u> machines — see p82-83) onto the chosen surface, e.g. a vehicle. It can also be used for creating <u>signs</u> and <u>stencils</u>.

CORRUGATED PLASTIC

Known as '<u>corriflute</u>', is <u>lightweight</u>, <u>rigid</u> and <u>weatherproof</u> corrugated plastic. It's often used for estate agents' sign boards, students' folders, etc.

FOR SALE
Trent, Reznor & co
020 7xxx-xxxx

corrugated plastic

HARD WAX

<u>Hard wax</u> has a crumbly texture. It is difficult to mould while dry, but can be melted down and reformed in a mould. It's used in the '<u>lost wax</u>' casting process.

Learn the uses of these thermoplastics

So, there are <u>thermoplastics</u> which can be remoulded and <u>thermosetting</u> plastics which can't. A lot of the thermoplastics have horrible long chemical names, so make sure you can spell them.

Plastics — Manufacturing Techniques

Plastic can be <u>shaped</u> or <u>moulded</u> in loads of different ways:

- You can heat it and bend it (<u>line bending</u>).
- It can be heated and sucked around a mould (<u>vacuum forming</u>).
- It can be heated and blown into a mould (<u>blow moulding</u>), heated and squeezed through a shaped hole (<u>extrusion</u>), or it can be heated and pushed into a hollow mould (<u>injection moulding</u>)...
  ...to name but a few.

Learn these *five* **plastic-forming methods**

1 Line Bending

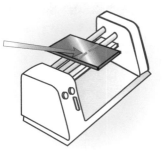

The heating element heats the material along the line where you want to bend it.

Line bending (<u>LB</u>) is ideal for use with <u>acrylic sheet</u> — for making picture frames and pencil holders, etc. It can be done <u>manually</u> or with a <u>jig</u> (a tool for cutting/making things accurately) to bend the plastic to a <u>specific angle</u>.

2 Vacuum Forming

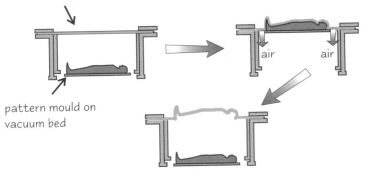

heated thermoplastic

air   air

pattern mould on vacuum bed

Vacuum forming (<u>VF</u>) is ideal for use with <u>rigid polystyrene</u> to make trays, casings and containers, e.g. chocolate box trays.

3 Blow Moulding

<u>Blow moulding</u> (<u>BM</u>) uses a <u>two-part mould</u> to make simple hollow objects, like containers for liquids. <u>Blow moulding</u> can also be used with glass, e.g. milk bottles.

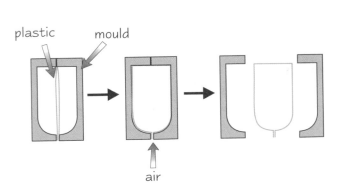

plastic   mould

air

Plastics — Manufacturing Techniques

4 Extrusion

Extrusion is ideal for making <u>simple</u>, <u>regular-shaped items</u> like guttering, drain pipes, etc., which can then be cut to a suitable length.

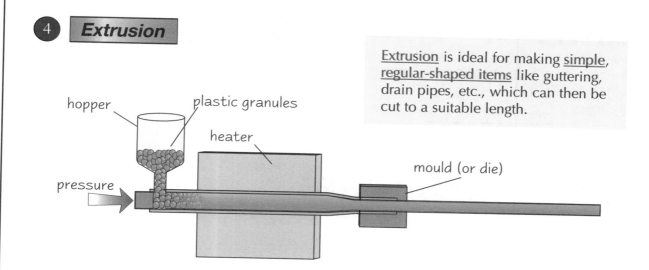

5 Injection Moulding

<u>Injection moulding</u> (IM) is ideal for making <u>complex</u> and <u>highly detailed components</u>, including model kits, seats, and 35 mm film canisters.

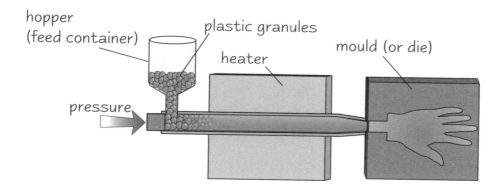

A 'die' is just another name for a mould

You heat up the plastic then form it into your product... easy. There are five plastic-forming methods to learn here. Make sure you can describe how each one works and name a product that you make with each one.

Smart Materials

Materials are called 'smart' or 'dumb' depending on whether they respond to a stimulus...

Smart

Materials that <u>respond to a stimulus</u> (e.g. a change in <u>heat</u>, <u>light</u>, <u>moisture</u> or <u>voltage</u>) can be described as '<u>adaptive</u>', '<u>active</u>', '<u>intelligent</u>' or '<u>smart</u>'.

Dumb

Materials that <u>do not</u> respond to a stimulus (like <u>wood</u> and <u>stone</u>) can be described as '<u>passive</u>' or '<u>dumb</u>'.

Smart plastics have clever properties

1) <u>Electro-luminescent panels</u> combine fluorocarbons and phosphorous to <u>produce light</u> (but not heat) when stimulated by <u>electricity</u>. Applications include light strips for decorating buildings.

2) <u>Lenticular plastic</u> is an <u>optically embossed film or sheet</u>. Viewed on its lenticular side, it can give the impression that the sheet is <u>thicker than it really is</u>. It's used to make optical effects, and pictures that appear to move when looked at from different angles. It looks a bit like a <u>hologram</u>.

3) <u>Liquid crystal displays</u> (<u>LCDs</u>) are made of a material which responds to <u>electrical signals</u>. LCDs are used to make calculator displays and laptop computer screens.

4) <u>Polycaprolactone</u> (sometimes called a <u>polymorph</u>) is a type of plastic used in <u>rapid prototyping</u> (making models to try out new designs). Its <u>low melting point</u> of 62 °C means that it can be made <u>mouldable</u> by immersing it in <u>hot water</u>. Polycaprolactone can be moulded and <u>shaped by hand</u> when warm, or <u>machined</u> when cold. When fully cooled, it looks similar to nylon and is stiffer and stronger than HDPE (see page 20).

If you use polycaprolactone, don't overheat it, or you'll ruin it.

Smart Materials

Smart wire 'remembers' its shape

Nitinol

- <u>Nitinol</u> is an <u>alloy</u> of <u>nickel</u> and <u>titanium</u>.

- It is one of a number of alloys that exhibit <u>shape-memory</u> characteristics — i.e. it can be made to <u>remember</u> a particular <u>shape or length</u> and <u>return</u> to it when a particular <u>temperature</u> or <u>voltage</u> is applied.

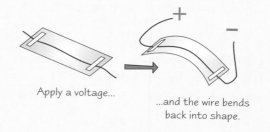

Apply a voltage...

...and the wire bends back into shape.

The uses of nitinol smart wire include braces for teeth, spectacle frames, valves, locks and robotic devices.

Smart wire shouldn't be overheated, or it'll stop working.

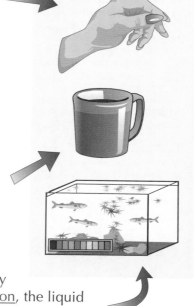

Smart dyes change in response to heat / light / water

1) <u>Photochromic dyes</u> change colour reversibly in response to <u>light</u>. Uses include nail polish, yo-yos, T-shirts, etc.

2) <u>Solvation-chromic dyes</u> change colour in response to <u>moisture</u>. Products under development include handkerchiefs, nappies and hygiene products.

3) <u>Thermochromic dyes</u> change colour reversibly in response to <u>changes in temperature</u>. Products include mugs, bubble bath, baby spoons, dishes and wine bottle labels.

4) <u>Thermochromic liquid crystal</u> changes colour reversibly in response to <u>heat</u>. By a process of <u>micro-encapsulation</u>, the liquid crystal is made into an <u>ink</u>, which can be printed onto a <u>substrate</u> (e.g. plastic or paper). Uses include battery test panels, warning patches on computer chips, and thermometers for fish tanks.

Nitinol — a smart wire with loads of uses

So, smart wire changes back to it's original shape due to temperature and voltage, and smart dyes change due to temperature, light and water. You need to know the examples well for the exam.

Smart Materials

Smart materials are used in loads of things you wouldn't think of...

Smart materials are used in lots of electrical products

1) <u>IQ Controllers</u> are low-cost self-contained units containing a chip capable of switching up to three outputs on and off in a pre-programmed sequence. They're used in school D&T work.

2) <u>PICs</u> (<u>Peripheral Interface Controllers</u>) are used to put a program onto a <u>microchip</u> to control a circuit. You might use them at school. PICs are used in industry and are embedded in phone cards and credit cards.

3) <u>Piezoelectric materials</u>, e.g. lead zirconate titanate (PZT) or lead lanthanite zirconate titanate (PLZT), produce <u>electrical energy</u> when a mechanical <u>force</u> is applied — and <u>vice versa</u>. They have a variety of applications, including speaker circuits (like you get in some greetings cards), inkjet printers, ignition switches and intruder alarms (the kind that send a signal to a control centre).

New modern materials are constantly being developed

Modern materials <u>enhance</u> the <u>performance</u> of a product. They replace (or are combined with) natural ingredients in food, and natural fibres in textiles. New <u>materials</u> are continually being developed through the invention of new or improved processes. These include:

1) Biological materials, such as <u>modified enzymes</u>, <u>antioxidants</u>, <u>synthetic flavours</u> and <u>genetically engineered foods</u>.

2) Strong materials such as <u>carbon fibre</u>, <u>KEVLAR® fibre</u> (KEVLAR® is used in bulletproof vests) and <u>composite materials</u>.

3) Materials for communication technology, e.g. <u>optical fibres</u>.

4) Materials for finishing processes, such as <u>Teflon®</u>.

Formula 1 car bodies are made of carbon fibre.

5) Materials for insulation and clothing, such as <u>neoprene</u>, <u>synthetic micro-fibres</u>, <u>LYCRA®</u> and <u>Polartec®</u>.

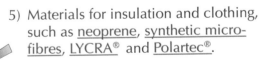

Divers' wetsuits are made from neoprene.

Modern materials... what will they think of next...

Smart materials have enabled manufacturers to improve existing products, as well as develop new ones. <u>Learn this page</u> — that's what it's for.

Fillers and Finishing

Finishes are things like <u>paint</u>, which are applied to a model or product to <u>protect</u> it from <u>damage</u> and <u>dirt</u> — and to improve its <u>appearance</u>. But before being painted or varnished, most surfaces need some kind of <u>filling or sanding</u>...

Fillers prepare surfaces for finishing

1) <u>Car-body filler</u> (David's Isopon) is a <u>two-part resin-based product</u>, which, when mixed, sets to a tough finish that can then be machined (i.e. drilled, filed, etc.).

2) <u>Polyfilla</u> is powder that's mixed with water to make a thick paste. This can <u>fill small cracks</u> and <u>improve the surface finish</u> on rough wood and foam models. It sets quickly and can be smoothed with glass paper.

3) <u>Plaster of Paris</u> is a fine white powder, which, when mixed with water, soon sets to a very hard finish. It's used with bandages to set broken limbs and to produce <u>landscape features</u> on <u>scale models</u>. It can be <u>cast in a mould</u>.

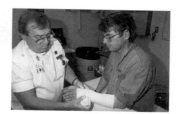

4) <u>Art Roc</u> or <u>Modroc</u> is a <u>bandage</u> material <u>impregnated with plaster of Paris</u>. It's great for creating textured landscape surfaces too, particularly when painted.

Laminating and varnishing makes your work look smarter

1) <u>Laminating</u> (or <u>encapsulation</u>) is a quick and effective way to finish a piece of work on paper or thin card. Laminating uses heat to <u>sandwich</u> the paper or card between <u>two layers of plastic</u> (see p53). This gives a professional finish to posters, menus, bookmarks, etc.

2) <u>Spirit varnish/lacquers</u> consist of a <u>synthetic (man-made) resin</u> (e.g. acrylic resin, cellulose resin) dissolved in an <u>organic solvent</u>. The solvent evaporates to leave a thin protective layer of varnish. Varnish/lacquer can be applied with a <u>brush</u> or <u>spray can</u>.

Paints are made from pigment dissolved in a 'vehicle'

1) <u>Paints</u> are made up of a <u>pigment</u> (a colour) and a '<u>vehicle</u>' (a solvent — something that <u>carries</u> the pigment).

2) There's a whole load of different 'vehicles', like <u>water</u>, <u>acrylic</u>, <u>cellulose</u>, <u>oil</u>, etc.

3) Once the paint has been applied, the vehicle <u>evaporates</u> to leave just the pigment.

4) Pigments may be made from chemicals, rocks or plants. <u>Woad</u>, which used to be used to dye <u>jeans</u> blue, comes from a <u>plant</u>.

5) Paints can be <u>brushed on</u>, or <u>sprayed on</u> from a can.

Several thin coats of paint, stain, varnish, etc. look better than one thick coat.

You can apply paint and varnish using a brush or using a spray can

Learn which <u>fillers</u> and <u>finishes</u> are best for <u>which surfaces</u>. You don't want to spoil a model that you spent ages on by messing up the finish.

Warm-up and Worked Exam Questions

Time to make sure you've learnt the stuff on materials before you move on to tools.
Ease yourself into it by answering the warm-up questions first.

Warm-up Questions

1) What name is given to paper that is very thin, translucent and suitable for design work?
2) When describing the weight of paper, what does 'gsm' stand for?
3) What class of plastics can be moulded/remoulded by heating?
4) What lightweight, crumbly plastic is well suited for protective packaging?
5) Which manufacturing technique should be used to make a moulded keyring?
6) What is a 'smart' material?

Read through the worked exam questions below before you answer the practice exam questions.
They'll help to give you an idea of how to answer exam questions.

Worked Exam Questions

1   A packaging company wants to be known to its customers as an 'environmentally friendly' company. They need to tell the customers about 'sustainability.'

 a)   Explain the term 'sustainable resource'.

This is when the source of the material is renewed naturally.

Examples include responsible tree planting and harvesting.

Because the question is worth 2 marks it's a good idea to give an example.   *(2 marks)*

 b)   Explain the term 'non-sustainable resource'.

The resource is finite, and will eventually be consumed.

(1 mark)

2   a)   Give two reasons why corrugated card is a good choice for secondary packaging.

It is recycled and recyclable.

It makes strong cartons for stacking.

(2 marks)

 b)   Give two reasons why corrugated plastic sheet (Corriflute) is suitable for an estate agent's sign.

It comes in all colours – different agents want different coloured boards.

It is a tough material, so it is not damaged easily by vandals or weather.

For this question it helps to think about where an estate agent might use a sign.   *(2 marks)*

Exam Questions

3   3D Solutions is the name of a manufacturing company.

    a)   3D Solutions want to make a single prototype plastic picture frame similar to the one below.

Which manufacturing technique should they use to bend sheet acrylic?

....

(1 mark)

    b)   3D Solutions also mass-produce plastic bottles for a bottled water company. Every month they have to make half a million plastic bottles. Which mass production manufacturing process should they use?

....

(1 mark)

    c)   3D Solutions have also been asked to update the appeal of a plastic toothpaste tube. This update is needed because the graphics and finish of the toothpaste tube are now seen as 'old fashioned'. 3D Solutions intend to solve this problem by using 'smart' and modern materials.

Name any two 'smart' or modern materials that could make the toothpaste tube more visually appealing.

....

....

(2 marks)

4   a)   Name one technique that could be used to add a glossy finish to a hotel menu card.

....

(1 mark)

    b)   Explain how the technique for a glossy finish you named in part (a) is achieved as an industrial process.

....

....

(2 marks)

Drawing and Painting Media

When designing and producing <u>presentation drawings</u> there are <u>loads of different media</u> you can choose from. Mixing your media can produce <u>stunning</u> results — so be daring and experiment.

Pencils are often used in design drawings

"You can lead a horse to water but a pencil must be lead." (Stan Laurel)

Pencils are classified by their <u>hardness</u> (<u>H</u>) and <u>blackness</u> (<u>B</u>) and range from <u>9H</u> to <u>9B</u>.
An <u>HB</u> pencil is in the middle as it's both hard and black, and is good for general sketching.
A harder pencil (like a <u>2H</u>) is better for precise, <u>technical drawings</u> as it won't smudge so easily.

1) Pencils are made from a mixture of <u>graphite</u> (a form of carbon) and clay.

The more graphite, the blacker (and softer) the pencil.

2) <u>Coloured pencils</u> come in a range of colours and a variety of hardnesses. The <u>softer</u> ones are best for laying <u>even</u>, <u>flat colour</u> and are less likely to <u>break</u>.

Inks, paints, pastels and dry-transfer lettering are also used

1) <u>Inks</u> are pigments suspended in water or solvent. They're good for <u>colour infilling</u>, <u>background washes</u> and <u>writing</u> (obviously).

Chalk pastels

2) <u>Gouache</u> is a type of <u>opaque paint</u>, which is ideal for producing <u>flat areas of colour</u>, or <u>highlights</u> on renderings (e.g. coats of plaster, mortar, etc.).

3) <u>Pastels</u> come in two varieties — <u>oil and chalk</u>. Pastels are particularly good for producing <u>backgrounds</u> on <u>renderings</u>, or adding <u>tone and shading</u>. It's easily blended using your fingers or cotton wool.

4) <u>Dry-transfer lettering</u> is applied with pressure from a waxed translucent sheet onto drawings or prototype models. It comes in various <u>typefaces</u>, <u>sizes</u>, <u>styles</u> and <u>colours</u>.

An HB pencil is the best all-rounder
For the <u>best results</u>, use the <u>best quality</u> pencils you can lay your hands on — you get what you pay for. Though I guess that goes without saying. Happy colouring in...

Drawing and Painting Media

Airbrushes blow a mist of ink

1) Airbrushes blow a fine mist of ink from a reservoir onto an image area, using compressed air from a compressor or a 'power pack' (can of compressed air).

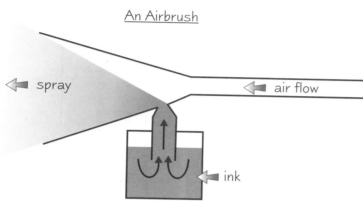

An Airbrush

spray

air flow

ink

2) It's a time-consuming medium — you have to mask all the areas you don't want to airbrush using a low-tack clear film and a craft knife. Plus you need loads of practice to do it well.

3) You can get really great photo-realistic results, if you know what you're doing. There are excellent examples of airbrushing on various record/CD sleeves, posters and adverts.

4) You should only airbrush in a well ventilated area so you don't inhale any ink. Ink isn't good for your lungs.

5) Airbrushing effects can also be achieved with some computer packages, e.g. Adobe® Photoshop®.

Felt pens and markers — water-based or spirit-based

Water-based pens aren't suitable for large areas because they dry quickly and leave streaks. Spirit based pens tend to produce better results but are more expensive. You can buy most pens in both forms. The ones you are most likely to use are:

1) Fine-liners come in a variety of thicknesses and colours. They're great for outlining drawings.

2) Markers are available in hundreds of different colour tones. They can have chisel, bullet and brush tips to offer greater flexibility of application. Popular brands include Magic Markers and Pantone®. Pantone® guarantee colour-matching across all their media — card, paper, paint, printing ink, etc. — meaning their 'dark green' paint is exactly the same colour as their 'dark green' card.

3) Technical pens are used for drawing fine, precise lines, e.g. orthographic drawings. They can be expensive and difficult to master.

Remember to airbrush in a well ventilated area
Sometimes pictures of fashion models are said to be airbrushed. This doesn't mean that they were sprayed with ink, but the image was tidied up (i.e. blemishes removed) using image editing software.

Drawing and Painting Equipment

Drawing things is much easier if you use the right equipment.

Drawing boards — *for easier, better drawing*

1) <u>Drawing boards</u> can be as simple as a sheet of blockboard or plywood.

2) The more sophisticated and expensive ones are <u>free-standing</u> and include a mechanism to adjust the angle of the board.

3) Some also include an integrated <u>parallel motion</u> or <u>T-square</u>.

Use *set squares*, *rulers* and *protractors* for marking angles

1) Set squares, as the name suggests, have angles which are set. The <u>30-60-90° set square</u> is pretty much essential for <u>isometric</u> and <u>planometric</u> projection. The <u>45-45-90° set square</u> is essential for <u>oblique</u> and axonometric <u>projections</u>. Both are useful for <u>orthographic</u> projection (see page 59).

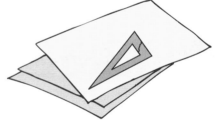

2) <u>Rulers</u> (or <u>rules</u>) are usually either 150 or 300 mm in length and made from steel, polypropylene or wood. They're used mainly for <u>measuring</u> and providing a <u>straight edge</u>. A steel <u>safety rule</u> is shaped so as to <u>protect the user's fingers</u> when cutting or scoring card and paper.

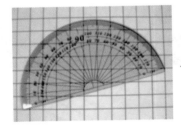

3) <u>Protractors</u> are used to <u>measure angles</u> in degrees. They're useful for drawing pie charts.

You need to clean set squares and T-squares regularly...

...or your work will get covered in smudges. To make sure that your drawings are accurate, you have to use set squares and rulers and things. You could guess angles, but it's best to use a protractor. Also, remember that it's easier to work on graphics if you're using a drawing board.

Drawing and Painting Equipment

Compasses draw circles and bisect lines

1) Compasses let you draw <u>accurate arcs</u> and <u>circles</u> of varying diameters.

2) They can also be used to <u>bisect</u> a line (divide it in half).

3) <u>Bow compasses</u> are more accurate than those with an attached pencil. <u>Beam compasses</u> allow <u>large</u> arcs and circles to be drawn.

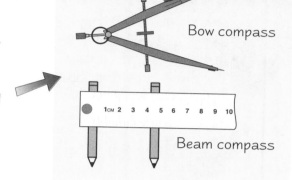

Bow compass

Beam compass

Curves and templates — for drawing curvy shapes

Curves and templates are used to <u>speed up</u> the drawing of <u>complex</u> and <u>repetitive shapes</u>.

1) <u>French curves</u> (or <u>ship's curves</u>) are curved templates used by designers to draw a variety of complex curves (and profiles for ships, hence the name).

French curve

2) <u>Flexicurves</u> are a variation on a French/ship's curve and can be shaped and <u>reshaped</u> to provide limitless profiles.

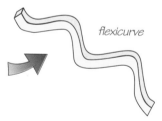

flexicurve

3) <u>Ellipse</u> and <u>circle templates</u> are used to quickly produce ellipses and circles of varying sizes.

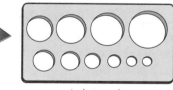

circle template

4) <u>Eraser guides</u> are used to protect a drawing while using an eraser to remove pencilmarks. Eraser guides make it easy to leave a highlight or tidy edge when erasing.

Templates and compasses make life a whole world easier

It's a good job you're not expected to draw <u>perfect straight lines</u> and <u>perfect circles</u> on your own. What a nightmare that'd be. So just remember to use all these bits of kit <u>when you need them</u>.

Adhesives

There are <u>loads</u> of different <u>adhesives and glues</u> to choose from. Each one's suited to a particular use or situation.

Here are the 10 types of **glue** you need to know

1) <u>Glue sticks</u> are commonly used in schools to bond paper and card as they're <u>non-toxic</u>, <u>cheap</u> and come in a range of handy sizes. Common brands include Pritt, UHU and Bostik. They're all clear when dry and are <u>environmentally friendly</u>.

2) Unlike glue sticks (which are solid), the glue sold in squeezy tubes (<u>glue pens</u>) is <u>liquid</u> and can be <u>messy</u> to use. Glue pens also bond paper and card and are clear when dry.

3) <u>Rubber-based cement</u> (or <u>gum</u>) is a <u>latex-based glue</u>. The glue should be applied to <u>both surfaces</u> and left for about ten minutes before bringing the surfaces together. <u>Repositioning</u> is possible.

4) <u>Aerosols</u> such as <u>3M Spray Mount</u>™ and <u>3M Photo Mount</u>™ cover large areas well and allow for <u>repositioning</u>. They're good for mounting photos onto paper or card — as the names might suggest. But they are highly flammable and must only be used in well ventilated areas.

5) <u>Superglue</u> comes in small tubes and quickly bonds a large variety of materials, e.g. ceramics, plastics, textiles and metal. It is often used in model making. If you're not careful you can stick your fingers together.

6) <u>Polyvinyl-acetate</u> (<u>PVA</u>) glue is a <u>water-based</u> glue used for bonding <u>wood</u>. It's also good for gluing paper and card, though it takes a while to dry.

7) <u>Epoxy resin glue</u> (e.g. <u>Araldite</u>®) is a <u>two-part</u> adhesive — with a <u>resin</u> and a <u>hardener</u>. 'Rapid' versions set in about 5 minutes, so speed is essential.

8) <u>Balsa cement</u>, as the name implies, is good for sticking <u>balsa wood</u>. It's clear when dry.

9) <u>Acrylic cement</u> (Tensol Number 12), as its name suggests, is used to bond <u>acrylic</u>. If you get it on your skin it can make it really dry and sore.

10) <u>Glue guns</u> are mains powered and use a <u>low-melt plastic</u> to quickly bond materials like <u>wood</u>, <u>fabric</u> and <u>card</u> together. The glue will <u>burn you</u> if it gets on your <u>skin</u>, so take care.

There's also **sticky-backed plastic, sticky tape** and **blu-tack**

1) <u>Sticky-backed plastic</u> can be used to <u>cover</u> and <u>protect</u> large awkwardly shaped card and paper models when <u>lamination</u> isn't possible.

2) Masking tape, Sellotape® and double-sided tape all come on <u>rolls</u>. <u>Masking tape</u> is <u>removable</u> low-tack tape, used to stick paper to drawing boards or to <u>mask</u> areas when using pastels or markers. Sellotape® is used for general sticking of card and paper. Double-sided tape is best used to stick <u>card models</u> and <u>shape nets</u>. It's good if you want the join hidden from view.

3) <u>Blu-tack</u> and white-tack are for <u>temporary fixing</u> — used mainly for sticking <u>posters to walls</u>, but also for <u>folder work</u> to allow for the <u>repositioning</u> of layouts.

The material you're working with affects which glue you use

Once again, there are simply loads of ways of doing something, and you have to figure out which one is best for what you're doing. You need to think how strong you want the adhesive to be and whether you want to permanently stick the two things together or whether you'll want to move them around.

Cutting Tools

There are many <u>cutting tools</u> available to manipulate <u>card</u> and <u>paper</u>, and make <u>models</u>. The following tools are ones you currently use, will use, or will need to know about.

Good old *scissors* cut *paper* and *thin card*

<u>Scissors</u> are probably the first cutting tool you ever used. They cut <u>paper</u> and <u>thin card</u> well, but are not suited to cutting <u>very fine detail</u> and <u>removing</u> bits from within a sheet of paper or card. Safety scissors have rounded ends and 'pinking shears' produce an interesting zigzag edge (which also helps stop material from fraying, so pinking shears are often used for things like fabric swatches).

Craft knives cut *card* and *paper*

There are loads of different <u>craft</u> / <u>trimming</u> / <u>hobby knives</u> on the market, and different schools use different types. Styles include <u>surgical scalpels</u>, <u>Stanley knives</u>, and other 'generic' types. Some have <u>retractable blades</u> or <u>blade covers</u> for <u>safety</u> when not in use. All are mainly used to cut card and paper, though some will cut thick board, balsa wood, etc.

Compass cutters cut *arcs* and *circles*

<u>Compass cutters</u> are used to cut arcs and circles in card and paper. Unlike a 'circle cutter' you can vary the diameter of the arc or circle to be cut. Use with a cutting mat.

Rotary cutters and *guillotines* cut *large sheets*

<u>Rotary cutters</u> (also known as rotatrims or paper trimmers) cut large sheets of paper and card, often <u>many sheets at a time</u>. They cut in a straight line to produce a nice straight edge. <u>Guillotines</u> do the same thing, but they have a large blade that you push down.

*Modelling materials need **special cutters***

You may wish to use styrofoam, thin plywood or MDF in your models. <u>STYROFOAM</u>™ is best cut with a <u>hot-wire cutter</u>. <u>Plywood</u> and <u>MDF</u> are easily cut using a <u>fret saw</u> or <u>coping saw</u>. A <u>Hegner saw</u> (a kind of jigsaw with a very thin blade) is a quicker option and gives excellent results with care.

*Die cutters and creasing bars **cut shapes***

<u>Die cutters</u> are commercial cutters (not unlike pastry cutters) which <u>cut out</u> materials for packaging. <u>Creasing bars</u> add <u>creases</u>, which makes the material easier to fold.

When using cutting equipment, always take appropriate safety precautions.

*Safety equipment is really **important***

A cutting mat

When using a <u>craft knife</u> or any sharp-bladed cutting tool, it's best to use a <u>cutting mat</u> (to protect your work surface) and a <u>safety rule</u> (to protect your fingers). When cutting <u>STYROFOAM</u>™ and <u>MDF</u>, make sure there's plenty of <u>ventilation</u> and extraction — and wear a mask.

A safety rule has a rubber back so it doesn't slip when you're cutting

<u>Take care</u> when cutting, you don't want to wreck your work or lose a finger. Make sure you measure and mark out areas to be cut. Once you've done that, <u>double check</u> your measuring just to make sure.

Tools and Materials

It's dead important to use the right tool for a job.
It makes it easier for you, and will mean the final result is better.

Cut **wood** with a **saw** — but choose the right kind

1) <u>Coping saw</u> — this small saw can be used to cut <u>wood</u> and <u>plastic</u> in curved and irregular shapes.

2) <u>Piercing saw</u> — this is very similar to a coping saw, but is quite weak due to its thin blade. It can also be used on <u>metals</u> and <u>plastics</u>.

3) <u>Tenon saw</u> — good for sawing materials to length, e.g. <u>dowelling</u>.

4) <u>Bench-mounted vibro saw</u> — this is an <u>electric</u> version of a piercing/coping saw. It's also used on <u>plastics</u>.

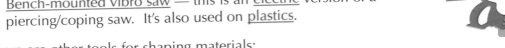

There are other tools for shaping materials:

- <u>Glasspaper</u> — this is used to put a very smooth surface finish on a <u>variety of materials</u>.
- <u>Surform tools</u> — there are a load of different handtools all under the heading "Surform" tools (it's a brand name). They include files and planes and they're used for shaping <u>wood</u> and <u>plaster</u>.

You might need **special tools** to work with **plastic**

1) <u>Vacuum former</u> — this machine moulds <u>polystyrene</u> to a desired shape using pre-made <u>patterns/formers</u> (see also page 22).

2) <u>Scraper</u> — this creates a smooth finish on the edges of <u>acrylic</u>, but it can also be used on <u>wood</u>.

3) <u>Wet and dry paper</u> — this is used after <u>filing</u> (first when the paper is dry, and then when it's wet) to achieve a very smooth finish. It can be used on <u>acrylic</u> and <u>metals</u> too.

4) <u>Hot-wire cutter</u> — this can be used on <u>expanded polystyrene foam</u> and <u>rigid foam</u> to shape with a smooth surface finish.

Metalwork also needs some **special tools**

1) <u>Files</u> — these are used to create a smooth finish on <u>metals</u> and <u>plastics</u>. A variety of shapes and tooth sizes are available.

2) <u>Needle files</u> — these are also used to create smooth finishes, but they're much finer and so are better for detailed work.

3) <u>Twist-drill bits</u> — these are for creating holes in <u>metal</u>, <u>wood</u> and <u>plastic</u>. They come in various sizes, and are used in <u>pillar</u>, <u>bench-mounted</u> or <u>hand drills</u>.

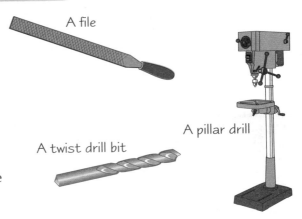

A file

A pillar drill

A twist drill bit

Files are great for making a smooth finish on metal and plastic

Picking the right tools for the right material is really important, e.g. it'll probably take you years to cut a bit of metal with a hot-wire cutter... and you'll probably spoil your work in the process.

Fixings

Fixings are for joining materials together. Some methods of fixing can join a number of different types of materials. There are also specific fixings designed to suit a particular material — e.g. corrijoints, which are bits of injection-moulded plastic used to join plastic corrugated board.

Learn about all these kinds of fixings

1) Ratchet rivets and rapid-assembly post and screw fixings are designed to join sheets of corriflute (corrugated plastic) together. Both fixings push together to form a secure joint.

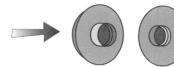

2) Eyelets are used to join pieces of card together whilst providing a movable joint. This is great for making card mechanisms, e.g. linkages (see also p95). The eyelets are applied using a special punch.

3) Prong paper fasteners are used to join pieces of paper and card together. The fastener is inserted through a hole and then opened out. Like eyelets, they can make movable joints for card mechanisms and linkages.

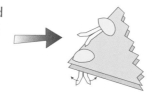

4) Paperclips are a temporary fixing for a number of pieces of paper or thin card.

5) Staples are a permanent or temporary fixing for a number of pieces of paper or thin card. Staples can be removed with a staple-remover.

6) Velcro® pads are self-adhesive pieces of the famous two-part hook and loop system. They have hundreds of different uses and are particularly good for display purposes.

7) Drawing pins (also known as thumb tacks or mapping pins) are useful for sticking paper and card to display boards.

8) Press stud fastenings are good for joining fabric bits together.

Have a look at home for uses of the different fixings

I bet you can find loads, e.g. press-studs on your duvet, eyelets on your curtains and velcro on your sofa cushions. In your exam you might be asked to say which fixing would be best to use for any given situation. So you know what that means... you're gonna have to learn them.

38

Ways of Producing Work

You can produce really impressive work using desktop publishing. It's also really handy to be able to copy the work you have done using photocopiers or tracing.

Desktop publishing is page layout by computer

1) Desktop publishing (DTP) is when you do newspaper, book and magazine layouts on a computer rather than by hand. DTP packages, like QuarkXPress®, Adobe® PageMaker® and Microsoft® Publisher, allow for increased speed and creativity. Ideas can be tried out and then changed in seconds.

2) DTP packages allow for multiple layers of colour and images to be created. They make it easy to add text which flows or 'wraps around' a photograph or image.

This book was laid out in Adobe® PageMaker®, by the way.

3) Images are usually imported into DTP packages from other programs, like Adobe® Photoshop®, Adobe® Illustrator® or CorelDRAW®.

Photocopiers are used to reproduce work

Photocopying is a 'dry' printing process. This means that no liquids are present — the ink (toner) is a powder, that 'bonds' to the paper when it's heated inside the machine.

Photocopiers have many functions. Many can:
1) enlarge and reduce an original image, up to A3 size,
2) print onto thin, textured paper, card or acetate,
3) automatically collate a number of documents — i.e. put the pages in the right order,
4) print double-sided,
5) print from double-sided documents,
6) punch holes and staple.

Use photocopiers to quickly and cheaply reproduce 'borders' for your project work or copy images from books and catalogues for use in development work.

Light boxes help to trace images accurately

Light boxes are exactly what you'd expect — boxes with a light in them...

1) Just put the image you want to trace on top of the light box, a piece of paper over that, and hey presto — you can see the original image really easily.
2) Tracing images is useful to copy parts of a design or plan quickly and accurately.

DTP is great for trying out new ideas...
If you have DTP software at school, get used to using it — it's really useful. Photocopiers and light boxes are there to help you produce work quickly and easily. Use them when you can.

Warm-up and Worked Exam Questions

Have a go at answering these warm-up questions. Remember to go back and check out anything you're unsure of before trying the practice exam questions.

Warm-up Questions

1) What is the purpose of a prototype model?
2) Pencils are graded H – B. What does 'B' stand for?
3) How is chalk pastel applied?
4) What name do we give to this piece of drawing equipment?

5) What are the names given to the two separate components of epoxy resin?

Now that you're suitably warmed up it's time for the practice exam questions. They're the best way to make sure you're prepared for the exam.

Worked Exam Questions

1   Camilla is a graphic designer working on a two part plastic pencil case. She wants to make a mould for the vacuum formed parts. The mould will be made from MDF.

   a)   What type of saw could she use for cutting along this straight line in 9mm MDF?

   A tenon saw.

   (1 mark)

   b)   After the MDF is cut, the sawn edge will be rough. How can it be made smooth?

   By using glass paper or a file.

   (1 mark)

2   To develop her design, Camilla wants to adapt an idea from a previous drawing.

   a)   What are the advantages of using a light box for tracing parts of this drawing?

   It's quick, easy and accurate.

   (2 marks)

If the question asks you to compare two things make sure you say something about both of the things.

   b)   To help her develop her idea for the shape of the pencil case, Camilla has a light box and photocopier. What is an advantage of each?

   A light box allows for design adaptation and development. A copier can be used enlarge or reduce the original design.

   (2 marks)

Exam Questions

3   Rory is a graphic designer who works for a large DIY superstore. He has been asked to make a 3D scale model of the kitchen. He is going to use expanded polystyrene foam.

   a)   What model making equipment should he use for cutting the foam blocks to size: 100 x 100 x 60 mm?

   ....

   (1 mark)

   b)   How can the foam blocks be permanently fixed onto a board?

   ....

   ....

   (2 marks)

   c)   The foam blocks will be fixed onto an MDF board with a curved edge. What type of saw is suitable for cutting along this curved line in 6mm MDF?

   ....

   (2 marks)

   d)   To advertise the kitchen manufacturer's name, a small amount of lettering is to be applied to the model's plastic work surface. Rory intends to use dry transfer lettering for this purpose.

   How is dry transfer lettering applied?

   ....

   ....

   (2 marks)

Revision Summary for Section Two

Do as you did for Section One — try to do all the questions and check back over the section to see if you got them right. It's a good way of finding out what you need to do more work on.

1) In what units are the weights of paper and card measured?

2) Describe duplex board, and say why it's used extensively in food packaging.

3) Describe the main difference between a thermoplastic and a thermosetting plastic.

4) What are the two main types of polyethylene? Describe their properties.

5) Why is expanded polystyrene used as a packaging material?

6) What is corriflute? Describe a couple of uses of this material.

7) Describe five plastic-forming methods.

8) With which plastic-forming method would you produce complex, highly detailed components?

9) Describe the properties of: a) electro-luminescent panels, b) polymorph.

10) Explain the properties of Nitinol, a smart wire. What is it used for?

11) Name three stimuli that smart dyes can respond to.

12) What are piezoelectric materials? In what products might you find them?

13) Name four fillers, and describe when they might be used.

14) Give two reasons why a finish might be applied to a product.

15) What is a 'vehicle', in terms of paint?

16) What two letters are used to classify pencils? What's the significance of each letter?

17) Why are water-based felt pens not suitable for covering large areas?

18) Explain when it might be a good idea to use a safety ruler.

19) Describe the properties and uses of:
a) glue sticks, b) rubber-based cement, c) superglue, d) PVA glue, e) epoxy resin glue.

20) Describe when you might use: a) a craft knife, b) a rotary cutter, c) a die cutter.

21) Name four types of saw, and describe their uses.

22) Explain when you might use a hot-wire cutter.

23) Name two types of fixing that allow you to make linkages in card.

24) Explain how Velcro® works.

25) Describe five things a modern top-of-the-range photocopier can do.

26) Describe how DTP packages have speeded up the process of producing publications.

What Designers Do

Graphic design is all about <u>communicating ideas</u> through <u>pictures</u>. This section's all about different ways of doing just that.

You can **communicate** ideas by drawing

1) Designers <u>communicate</u> their ideas through drawings.
2) The drawings include <u>notes</u> and <u>annotations</u> to explain details.
3) They're used in <u>meetings</u> with clients to explain concepts.

Prototypes are models of the product

1) Prototypes are sometimes referred to as <u>mock-ups</u>.
2) They're produced to <u>explain a concept</u> in 3-D.
3) Producing a prototype makes sure the designs are fully <u>understood</u>.
4) They're usually produced <u>to scale</u>.

Find a **gap in the market** to promote a new product

1) Before launching a new product, you need to find a <u>gap in the market</u>.
2) This is an area where, at present, there's no product available to meet the <u>customers' needs</u>.
3) The new product then needs to be <u>promoted</u> in a way that looks <u>attractive</u> to the <u>target customer</u>, this is known as <u>target marketing</u>.

Advertising needs to **attract** the customer

1) There are many <u>different techniques</u> used to <u>promote</u> a new product.
2) They include following <u>trends</u> in <u>fashion</u>. This encourages the customer to buy the product in order to appear <u>trendy</u> and up to date.
3) When a friend has bought a product, <u>peer pressure</u> may influence you to buy the product too.

Once you've got an idea, you need to communicate it

You can't just start building as soon as you've had an idea. You need to <u>design it</u> on paper first, thinking about <u>all the details</u>. Then make a <u>prototype</u> to see exactly how it'll look and work.

Sketching

You <u>don't always</u> have to use <u>perfect</u> drawings. <u>Freehand sketches</u> are fine for getting across <u>initial ideas</u>. And they're much <u>easier</u> to do, so you can get <u>new thoughts</u> on paper <u>quickly</u>.

Freehand sketching is very *quick*

1) <u>Freehand drawing</u> is where you <u>don't</u> use any <u>drawing equipment</u> apart from a pencil or pen.

2) It's the <u>quickest</u> method of illustration and is handy for getting <u>initial ideas</u> down on paper.

3) <u>3-D</u> freehand sketches often show how the <u>whole object</u> would look, while <u>2-D</u> drawings tend to show the <u>details</u> of an object.

Always start *2-D sketches* with *rectangles* and *squares*

Standard <u>sketching</u> is very similar to <u>freehand</u> sketching, except that you start by <u>ruling guidelines</u>.

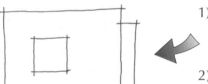

1) Using <u>vertical</u> and <u>horizontal</u> lines you can create squares and rectangles.

2) Use these to draw the <u>outline</u> of your shape first.

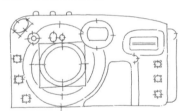

3) Details can be added by drawing more <u>squares</u> and <u>rectangles</u>.

4) Add <u>circles</u> and <u>ellipses</u> where necessary.

You need to be able to draw shapes accurately in the exam, so make sure you know basic shapes like octagons and how to draw them.

1) <u>Circles</u> are drawn in <u>square</u> boxes and <u>ellipses</u> are drawn in <u>rectangular</u> boxes.
2) Mark <u>half way</u> along each side.
3) <u>Join the points</u> to form the circle or ellipse.

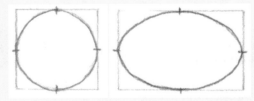

If you get a good idea, quickly sketch it... then fill in the details later
Remember to always start by drawing the outline of the object. Keep checking the proportions and don't start adding the details until you're sure all the bits are the right size and shape.

Sketching

3-D sketches are a little more complicated than 2-D sketches...

3-D sketches are done using crating

Crating is drawing where you start by drawing a box, or 'crate', then gradually adding bits on and taking bits off till you get the exact shape.

1) When you're sketching a 3-D object, it's easier if you imagine it as a basic shape.

2) First you draw the basic geometric shape faintly.

3) Try to stick to a particular drawing technique like 2-point perspective or isometric.

4) The object can then be drawn within the box.

5) Details of the object can be added by drawing more geometric shapes on top.

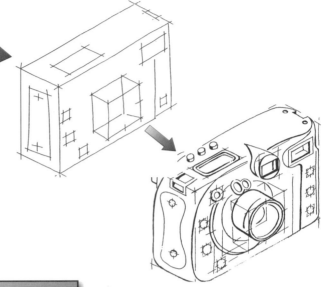

Any 3-D shape can start out as a cuboid

You can use a cuboid to draw other 3-D shapes:

1) Draw a cuboid.
2) Mark the sides of the cuboid halfway along (depending on what shape you want).
3) Draw the base and the top of the shape as 2-D objects.
4) Join up the two shapes.

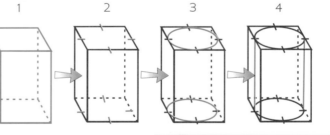

If you have a shape with a pointy top (e.g. a pyramid, or a cone), make a cross at the top of the cuboid and draw the point going to the middle of the cross.

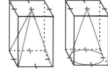

You can also cut sections out of the cuboid to produce other shapes.

Spheres and ellipsoids are different — they can't be made from cuboids.

1) They are circles and ellipses that are shaded to look 3-D.

2) The circles and ellipses are drawn using the 2-D technique.

To draw more accurately use a grid

1) Grids can be laid under your page to improve the accuracy of your drawing. (Or you could just draw on graph/ grid paper.)

2) You could use an isometric grid, perspective grid or a square grid.

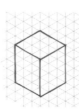

isometric

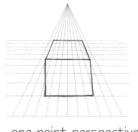

one-point perspective

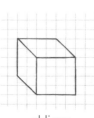

oblique

Sketching

A designer would use a combination of 2-D and 3-D sketches to communicate their ideas.

Wireframe drawings aren't shaded

1) When you draw using the <u>crating technique</u> (see opposite page), you can leave the solid sides of the shape <u>unshaded</u>.

2) Doing this lets you see <u>straight through</u> the object.

3) You can also view an object in <u>wireframe</u> in <u>CAD software</u>, like the camera shown here.

4) This could be used to show details on <u>all faces</u> of an object.

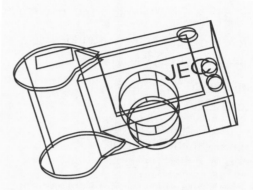

Develop ideas with sketches

1) Freehand sketching's <u>very quick</u> (as you know from p43).

2) You can <u>combine</u> <u>2-D</u> and <u>3-D</u> sketches to explain details.

3) And you can add <u>notes</u> to explain details further.

Remember to start 3-D objects with crates and cuboids...

If you find it hard to get the shapes just right, then try using grid paper. When you're developing ideas for a product, don't forget to scribble down notes and explanations next to your sketches — they'll show how you reached your final design.

Enhancement — Shading

You can use various techniques to <u>enhance</u> a drawing.
You can change the <u>thickness of lines</u> or add <u>shading</u> to make parts of the drawing <u>stand out</u>.

Pencil shading can be used to **accentuate shape**

1) <u>Shading</u> can be added to a shape to make it look <u>3-D</u>.

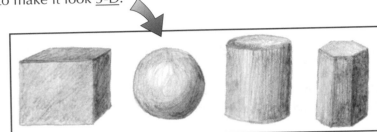

2) Different <u>pencils</u> can be used to create different <u>tones</u>.

3) A <u>soft pencil</u> will create a <u>wider tonal variation</u>.

4) Shading a drawing to show depth, light and shade or texture is called <u>rendering</u>.

5) Think about where the light's coming from — make areas furthest from the light the darkest.

You can use a pencil to **shade** *in* **different ways**

1) You can <u>shade shapes</u> using a normal <u>pencil</u> in a number of different ways.

2) Using different types of shading is useful for differentiating <u>parts</u> of an object.

1) When you shade using <u>dots</u>, you need to use a <u>different concentration</u> of dots on each side. Dot-matrix printers use this method, but it's fairly <u>time-consuming</u> by hand.

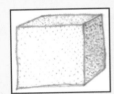

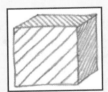

2) In order to shade using <u>lines</u>, you need to use <u>lines at different spacing</u> on each side. Lines at <u>different angles</u> can be used to show different colours, materials, etc.

3) Here's a quick and easy method to give the impression of <u>solidity</u>: If you can see <u>both surfaces</u> that form a line, draw it <u>thin</u>. If you can only see <u>one surface</u>, draw a <u>thick line</u>.

4) <u>Highlights</u> are used to suggest a highly <u>reflective</u> surface. They can be added by leaving <u>white</u> areas.

Shading is a great way to make objects look 3-D

This shading stuff's great fun. But you should expect that — this *is* Graphic Products, not <u>maths</u>. Don't get lost in the wave of pleasure this page brings you — you still need to <u>learn</u> and <u>practise</u> it all.

Enhancement — Surfaces and Textures

When shading shapes you can also use different techniques to represent different materials — e.g. adding underline textures, varying the underline tone and underline colour, etc.

You can use *colour* and *shading* to represent *surfaces*

Wood — *use colour and draw a grain...*

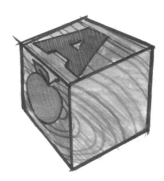

1) Wood can be done using underline coloured pencils to represent the colour and underline grain.

2) You can use more than one colour to get the underline right shade.

3) underline Wood grain can be added using a underline darker pencil. Remember that the underline side grain and the underline end grain look different.

Metal — *if it's shiny, draw the reflections...*

1) underline Metals can have a variety of colours and finishes.

2) You could have flat underline sheet metal, or metal with a underline texture.

3) When shading underline shiny metal you must be aware of underline highlights. Try looking closely at a piece of shiny metal in the light. What do the reflections actually look like?

4) underline Textured metal can be represented using underline line techniques, e.g. drawing lines to show any ridges, bumps etc.

Plastic — *here's a few tricks of the trade...*

1) underline Marker pens can be used to create the effect of underline plastic. Alternatively you could use soft underline coloured pencils or underline poster paints.

2) underline Pale coloured marker pens, watercolour paints or pencils or coloured pencils can be used to make an object appear underline transparent. You may even see objects through the transparent object.

3) Most dark colours look opaque automatically, but you could make a underline pale coloured material look underline opaque using underline watercolour paints by adding a bit of yellow.

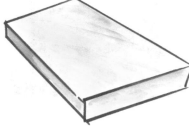

Remember — *shading adds texture to a picture*

Once you've got the hang of highlights, don't restrict yourself to only using them on metals. Anything shiny — glass, smooth plastic or any polished surface — will pick up highlights as well.

Enhancement — Colour and Mood

The use of <u>colour</u> is very important when producing drawings.
As well as being used to make a product <u>aesthetically</u> pleasing, it can be used to <u>represent mood</u>.

Colours can be organised into different groups

1) There are two main types of colour:
   <u>primary</u> and <u>secondary</u>.

2) The primary colours (<u>red</u>, <u>blue</u> and <u>yellow</u>) can
   be mixed together to produce <u>any</u> other colour.

3) <u>Secondary colours</u> are colours made by <u>mixing</u>
   together primary colours.

4) Colour can be represented on a <u>colour wheel</u>
   which shows you how all the colours fit together.

primary colours: red, yellow and blue

secondary colours: orange, purple and green

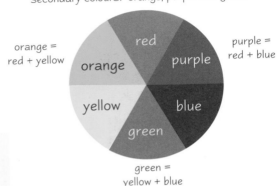

orange =
red + yellow

purple =
red + blue

green =
yellow + blue

N.B. This colour wheel only applies to paint or pigments — not to
light. The primary colours for light are red, green and blue, which
gives a different set of secondary colours as well.

Complementary colours are on opposite sides of the wheel

1) <u>Complementary</u> or <u>contrasting</u> colours are found
   <u>opposite</u> each other on the <u>colour wheel</u>.

2) Examples are red and green, blue and orange, yellow and purple.

3) In <u>CAD</u> packages (see p.52) you can <u>select colours</u> and
   also <u>edit</u> colours to specific requirements.

4) '<u>Hue</u>' is another word for 'colour'. It's used a lot in drawing software, e.g. CorelDRAW®,
   Adobe® Photoshop®.

Colours can be used to represent mood

1) Different colours can represent different <u>moods</u> or <u>feelings</u>.

2) To create a <u>heavy</u> mood, you might
   use a <u>dark solid colour</u> while for a
   <u>lighter</u> mood you'd go for a <u>paler colour</u>.

E.g. cartoon villains are often very dark colours
to give them a sinister feel, whereas the heroes
are light, bright colours which gives a happier, less
serious feel to the character.

3) <u>Hot</u> is usually represented by <u>reds</u>
   or <u>oranges</u>, whereas <u>blues</u> are
   normally associated with <u>cold</u>.

4) Colours can also represent the <u>mood</u>.
   For example <u>green</u> is often associated
   with <u>calm</u> or relaxation, while <u>red</u>
   often represents <u>anger</u> and conflict.

Think carefully about the colours you pick...

...they could create the wrong mood, e.g. a black wedding card wouldn't go down very well.
Also, make sure the colour is appropriate for the product — e.g. you wouldn't make a life raft the
same colour as the sea, you'd make it a bright colour so it'd be easy to spot by rescuers.

Enhancement — Colour in Print

There are two common <u>sets</u> of colours used in print — <u>RGB</u> and <u>CMYK</u>. They have different uses.

Traditional *television* screens use *three basic colours*

1) All pictures on a <u>television screen</u> are made from the colours <u>red</u>, <u>green</u> and <u>blue</u> (RGB colours).

2) The screen is made up of thousands of tiny coloured <u>dots</u> (<u>pixels</u>).

3) Each tiny pixel consists of a <u>red</u>, <u>green</u> and <u>blue</u> bar or dot. The intensity of each of these bars (or dots) produces the final pixel colour you see.

Colour printers use a different system

1) Colour printers use <u>cyan</u>, <u>magenta</u>, <u>yellow</u> and <u>black</u> (CMYK) as their key colours. (The 'K' stands for 'key' — it means black.)

2) Anything that's printed in colour is made up of a <u>mixture</u> of these colours. But usually you can't see this because the dots are so small and close together that your eyes can only see them fused together.

3) When the computer is instructed to print, the printer recognises the required colour and adds <u>layers</u> of cyan, magenta, yellow and black to make the final colour.

4) Some PC printers use <u>extra colours</u> as well as CMYK to make the image look more realistic — especially things like flesh tones in photos of people.

5) <u>Newspapers</u> and the like are printed as loads of little <u>dots</u> of colour — usually 150 dpi (dots per inch). You can see them if you look really closely.

You can make black by mixing the other three colours, but using black ink usually looks better, and works out cheaper if you're printing a lot of black.

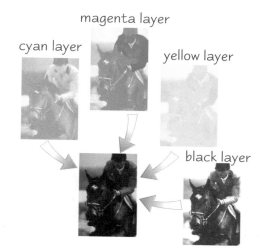

magenta layer

cyan layer

yellow layer

black layer

Screen printing uses a *similar system*

1) When screen printing, you also add colour in <u>layers</u>.

2) These layers build up to produce the final colour.

3) This is the traditional system of colouring <u>paper</u> and <u>cloth</u>.

4) An example of printing using layers is <u>newspapers</u>, where you can often see a colour bar showing the colours used.

The screen is made of a very fine mesh with a stencil on it. The mesh is held taut around a strong wooden frame. To print a design, you put a load of dye cream onto the mesh, then pull across a rubber squeegee to push the dye through the holes. And you get a pretty pattern on your T-shirt.

RGB for TVs and computer screens, CMYK for printers... easy

Primary colours can be a confusing subject. When you're mixing paints or inks, the primary colours are <u>subtractive</u>. With subtractive colours, if you mix all three you end up with <u>black</u>. Light on the other hand is <u>additive</u> which means mixing them all gives you <u>white</u>. That's what happens in TVs.

Paper Sizes, Mounting, Fixatives

Paper comes in all different shapes and sizes. You need to learn the standard sizes of paper so that you can talk about them at dinner parties. And at school.

There are many **standard paper sizes**

1) Paper sizes go from A0 (which has an area of 1 m²) to A1, A2, and so on — halving in size (area) each time.

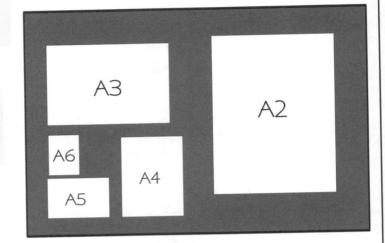

2) The most common paper sizes used in UK schools are A4 and A3. A4 is 297 mm × 210 mm, in case you're interested.

3) Many other sizes are also available:
   - A4 paper is half the size of A3 paper.
   - A5 paper is half the size of A4 paper.
   - A6 paper is half the size of A5 paper.

As the paper gets smaller the number increases.

The width of A3 paper is the length of A4.

The length of A3 paper is double the width of A4.

4) If the page is tall, it's referred to as 'portrait', whereas if it's wide, it's called 'landscape'.

portrait

landscape

Just remember A0 is huge and A6 is tiny...

...then you can work out all the other sizes in between. You will probably use A4 and A3 a lot at school.

Paper Sizes, Mounting, Fixatives

Once you've done your work on paper you're going to want to do something with it...

You can make **booklets** from **sheets** of paper

1) <u>Booklets</u> can be made by <u>folding</u> sheets of paper.

2) If <u>A4</u> paper is used and <u>folded in half</u> it creates 4 sides or <u>pages</u> which are <u>A5</u> size.

3) Booklets can be <u>stapled</u> to hold the separate sheets together.

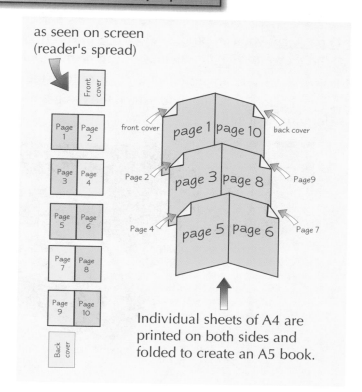

as seen on screen (reader's spread)

Individual sheets of A4 are printed on both sides and folded to create an A5 book.

Cardboard mounts can be made to **frame** a picture

1) You can make a <u>mount</u> to <u>frame</u> your picture using a piece of <u>cardboard</u>.

2) You need to choose an appropriate size of card and cut a hole in the <u>middle</u>.

3) The hole is usually positioned slightly <u>higher</u> than the <u>middle</u> of the picture, to help <u>balance</u> it.

4) Before you frame your picture, it's important to <u>protect</u> it.

5) Using a <u>fixative</u> spray or paint, you can protect your picture from <u>smudging</u> or <u>fading</u>.

Remember to fix your pictures or else they'll smudge...

...especially pictures drawn in chalk, charcoal or pastels. The dustier the medium you use, the more likely it is that you will need to protect it. Pictures are also framed to protect them.

CAD/CAM

CAD stands for <u>Computer-Aided Design</u> — it's the process of <u>designing</u> using a <u>computer</u>.
CAM stands for <u>Computer-Aided Manufacture</u> — using <u>machines</u> to make designs created on a computer.

CAD images can be *changed* to suit the customers' *needs*

1) Using <u>CAD packages</u> you can produce <u>drawings</u> of a <u>concept</u> or product.

2) In order to show <u>specific details</u>, the images can be manipulated in a number of ways.

3) You could show details of <u>dimensions</u>, <u>materials</u> or how the final product will appear.

4) This enables the customer to <u>fully understand</u> the designs and specify any changes before manufacturing.

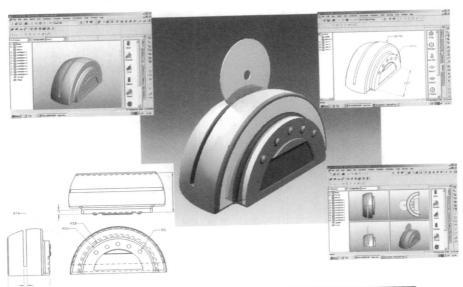

Examples of CAD drawings using Pro/DESKTOP software

Lettering can be *added* to products using CAD/CAM

1) Lettering varies from <u>ornate</u>, <u>traditional</u> styles to <u>modern</u>, <u>dynamic</u> styles.

2) Different lettering styles (fonts) are used for different <u>purposes</u>.

3) A <u>traditional</u> style wouldn't really be suitable for a <u>trendy</u>, new, up-to-date product.

4) In the same way, very <u>modern</u> styles may look out of place on some things like <u>greetings cards</u>.

5) Lettering can be created by <u>hand</u> or using <u>CAD</u>.

6) Lettering designed using a <u>CAD package</u> can be sent to a <u>CAM machine</u>, e.g. a vinyl cutter, to be produced.

7) This lets you make a very <u>accurate</u> product.

8) <u>Typography</u> is the <u>design</u> and <u>layout</u> of lettering or typefaces (characters).

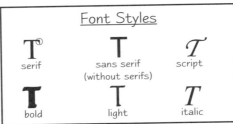

Font Styles

T serif	**T** sans serif (without serifs)	*T* script
T bold	T light	*T* italic

There are loads of fonts to choose from...

Different fonts really do make a difference to how people see things. Choosing the right one is really important. This is a very formal font. This is quite a 'fun' font. *This makes me think of medieval-type things.*

Protecting Paper Products

Sometimes it's really important to <u>protect</u> photographs, images and graphics to make sure they're <u>not damaged</u> easily.

Paper is very fragile

1) Paper is <u>easily damaged</u> by water and damp environments.
2) <u>Protecting</u> a paper product can extend its useful life.
3) Examples of products that may need protecting are <u>menus</u>, <u>instruction leaflets</u> and <u>signs</u>.

You can **cover** the paper to form a layer of **protection**

1) Paper products can be protected by <u>encapsulating</u> (enclosing) them in <u>sealed pockets</u>.

2) This is done using a <u>laminating machine</u>.

3) The paper product is <u>laid between</u> two sheets of clear plastic.

4) This sandwich is then inserted into the laminating machine, which <u>heats</u> the plastic and <u>seals</u> in the paper.

5) In industry, brochures can be laminated on one or both sides using gloss or matt laminate.

For **security**, photographs and names are **encapsulated**

1) <u>Passports</u>, security <u>identity badges</u> and <u>driving licences</u> use photographs to identify authorised people.
2) A <u>protective</u> film is added in order to ensure that the <u>photos</u> are not <u>damaged</u> or <u>changed</u> in any way.
3) Sometimes items are <u>encapsulated</u> to ensure that components are not <u>lost</u> or <u>damaged</u>, e.g. magazines with inserts sent through the post. This process is known as <u>polywrapping</u>.

Laminating and polywrapping — paper protection

So, that's "protecting paper products" for you. Laminating is a really handy thing — if you spill your cup of tea all over your work it won't get ruined. Don't forget polywrapping also protects paper and it's great for keeping loose paper and booklets together too.

Recording Stages Using Photography

Photographs are an alternative way of recording information about products or images.
They can be used for research purposes or through the designing stage to record developments.

Take photographs as *primary evidence*

1) You can take photographs to record the original problem.

2) It's worth taking photographs of other things that you'll need to think about during the design process, like the target user.

3) These images can then be stored and used later.

4) If a digital camera is used, the images can be stored on computer and used in presentations and reports.

5) There's also software that lets you play around with digital images to suit individual requirements. For example, colours can be adjusted to show how a product would look with different finishes.

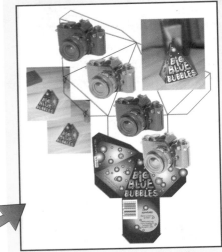

Montage of images using Photoshop

Record your work using *photographs*

1) Photographs can be used to record all intermediate stages of the design process, from research through to final outcome and testing.

2) These make a useful record of what's been achieved.

3) The photos can then be used in presentations about the product or to introduce new ideas.

Taking photographs at every stage of designing is a good idea

Digital photos are really useful because you can store them safely on your PC, then if something happens to your paper copy, you can just print another one. If you don't have a digital camera, you can always scan your paper photographs onto a computer.

Warm-up and Worked Exam Questions

You probably know the routine by now — do the warm-up questions first to check your basic knowledge before attempting the practice exam questions.

Warm-up Questions

1) What is the purpose of a prototype?
2) What name is given to colours that are opposite each other on the colour wheel?
3) What font style has been given to the letter T below?

T

If only all exam questions came with the answers already filled in. Unfortunately the examiners aren't that nice, so here's some more worked exam questions for you.

Worked Exam Questions

1 a) Use differently spaced lines to show 3 different types of shades on this cuboid.

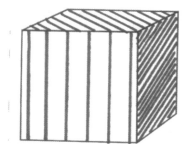

Make sure that any shading or sketches you do are nice and clear.

(2 marks)

   b) Name the technique that has been used to draw this diagram.

   Oblique.

(1 mark)

2 a) On a computer screen or TV, what three colours are used to create natural looking full colour?

   Red, green and blue.

(3 marks)

   b) What name do we give to a dot or square of colour on a computer screen?

   Pixel or picture element.

(1 mark)

3 A shop window sign needs to be made in sticky back vinyl. Give 2 advantages of designing the sign in a CAD application.

   It means the sign can be modelled and previewed in different colours.

   It can also be sent for CAM manufacture.

(2 marks)

56

Exam Questions

4   BTG is a printing company specialising in the production of booklets. They have been asked to produce an A5 size booklet with 16 pages. BTG intend to print on both sides of A4, then fold the A4 print in half, to make the A5 booklet.

a)   Using the above method, how many A4 sheets will be needed to make a 16 page, A5 booklet?

....

(1 mark)

b)   The booklet will be printed in full colour, using the four process colours. What are the four process colours?

....

(4 marks)

c)   i)   Describe how the process colours are combined on the print.

....

....

(2 marks)

ii)   Explain why individual process colours are not visible when printing certain colours, e.g. flesh tones.

....

....

(2 marks)

5   BTG also do CAD/CAM work.

a)   Suggest why BTG have invested in CAM equipment.

....

....

(2 marks)

b)   Give two advantages of CAM when design changes to a prototype are needed, in comparison to hand-made prototypes.

....

....

(2 marks)

Revision Summary for Section Three

Do the same as you did for Sections One and Two — try all these questions and find out how much you've learned. You can look back at the relevant bit of the section if you get stuck, but keep doing them till you can answer every single question without looking back.

If you can't do these questions, you don't know everything you need to know. Simple as that.

1) What is a prototype and why are they made?

2) Why is it important to find a 'gap in the market' before designing and launching a new product?

3) Suggest one way that you could attract a potential customer to a new product.

4) What are freehand sketches useful for?

5) How would you draw a circle or ellipse to the correct proportions when sketching?

6) How could you draw a simple 3-D sketch?

7) How and why would you use a grid when sketching?

8) Why might you want to view an object in wireframe?

9) What does the term 'rendering' mean?

10) Give four different shading techniques that you could use to make an object appear 3-D. Draw a cube to illustrate each of these methods.

11) Draw three 3-D shapes and shade them to look like wood, metal and plastic respectively.

12) Draw two 3-D shapes. Shade one to appear transparent and the other opaque.

13) For paints/pigments, what colours are classed as primary colours and which are the secondary colours?

14) What are complementary colours? Give three examples of complementary pairs.

15) What does 'hue' mean?

16) What colour is usually associated with anger and what colour is associated with cold?

17) What colours are used in a television screen? How does each pixel change colour?

18) What colours do colour printers usually use?

19) Give an example of a product that has been printed. How are the colours produced?

20) How big is A3 paper compared to A4 paper?

21) If you were making a booklet by folding A4 paper in half, how big would the booklet be?

22) Explain, using drawings and notes, how you could mount a picture and protect it from smudging.

23) Using CAD to produce designs, what information can you show a client?

24) What style of lettering would be suitable for labels on a trendy new electrical product, e.g. an MP3 player, and how could this lettering be produced using CAD/CAM?

25) How could you protect a photo or image from being damaged in a damp or moist environment?

26) How can photos be used throughout the design process?

Pictorial Drawings

When you draw pictures you can use different perspectives to make them look more realistic.

Perspective drawing — using *vanishing points*

1) <u>Perspective drawing</u> tries to show what something actually looks like — smaller in the distance, larger close to. It does this by using lines that appear to meet at points called <u>vanishing points</u>.

2) These points are in the distance on the <u>horizon line</u>.

3) There are two types of perspective commonly used — <u>one-point</u> and <u>two-point</u> perspective.

One-point perspective — for drawing objects **head on**

1) <u>One-point perspective</u> uses only <u>one vanishing point</u>.

2) The <u>front</u> view of an object is drawn <u>head on</u>.

3) <u>Lines</u> are then drawn to the <u>vanishing point</u> on the <u>horizon line</u>.

You've probably seen one-point perspective in cartoons without even realising it...

Use a <u>grid</u> to help to draw in proportion.

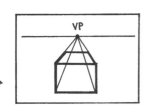 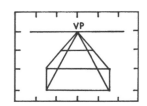 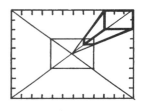

Two-point perspective — for objects at an **angle**

1) <u>Two-point perspective</u> gives a more <u>realistic</u> view of an object drawn at an <u>angle</u>.

2) The <u>horizon line</u> is drawn <u>horizontally</u> across the page.

3) <u>Two vanishing points</u> are marked on the horizon line.

4) The object is drawn by starting with the front edge and then <u>projecting lines</u> to the vanishing points.

5) Remember that <u>vertical</u> lines <u>remain vertical</u> and all <u>horizontal</u> lines go to the <u>vanishing points</u>.

The <u>position</u> of the <u>eye level</u> affects how the object appears.

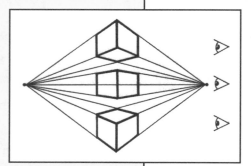

<u>Above</u> the horizon line

<u>On</u> the horizon line

<u>Below</u> the horizon line

Pictorial Drawings

Planometric drawings are useful for things like room layouts

As the name might suggest the <u>first</u> thing to draw with a <u>plan</u>ometric drawing is the <u>plan view</u>.

1) Draw the <u>plan view</u> to scale.
2) Then turn the plan view through <u>45°</u> or <u>30°</u>.
3) <u>Project</u> the vertical lines and <u>complete</u> the objects.
4) This gives a clear <u>three dimensional</u> impression of the object.

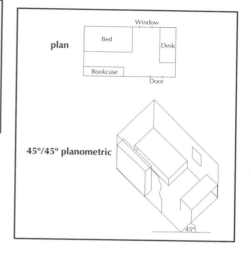

45°/45° planometric

Isometric drawing shows objects at 30°

1) Isometric drawing can be used to show a <u>3-D picture</u> of an object.

2) It <u>doesn't show perspective</u> (things don't get smaller in the distance), but it's easier to get dimensions right than in perspective drawing.

3) There are <u>three main rules</u> when drawing in isometric:

1. Vertical lines remain vertical.
2. Horizontal lines are drawn at 30°.
3. All lines are parallel on regular objects.

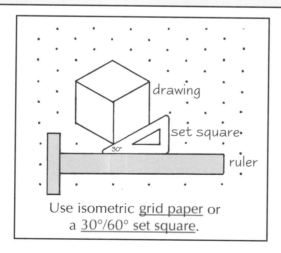

Use isometric <u>grid paper</u> or a <u>30°/60° set square</u>.

Try drawing in both 1-pt and 2-pt perspective to get the hang of it

Confused over which one to use when? OK, quick summary then: perspective drawing is more realistic (2-pt is more lifelike than 1-pt), but isometric drawing is easier (if you use isometric paper).

Working Drawings

Working drawings are for explaining to a production team how to make a product.
They include details on sizes, materials and assembly.

3rd angle orthographic projection (2-D views to you and me)

1) Orthographic projection shows
2-D views of a 3-D object.

2) All details are shown so the product can
be made to the designer's requirements.

3) The front view, plan view and end view of
the product are drawn accurately to scale.

4) The symbol for 3rd angle
orthographic projection is: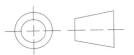

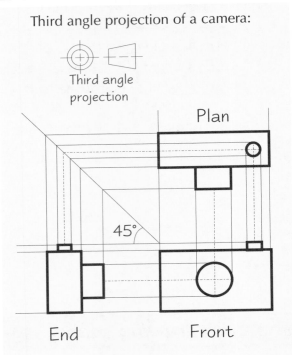

Third angle projection of a camera:

Third angle projection

5) To avoid confusion, lines and dimensions must
conform to the following British Standards
recommendations:

outlines: thick and continuous
projection/construction lines: light and continuous
centre lines: alternate short and long dashes, light
hidden details: short dashes, light
dimension lines: medium and continuous

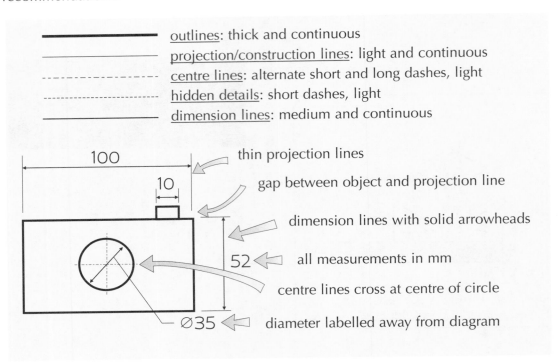

thin projection lines

gap between object and projection line

dimension lines with solid arrowheads

all measurements in mm

centre lines cross at centre of circle

diameter labelled away from diagram

Working Drawings

You need assembly drawings to put products together and plans to see where everything goes...

Assembly drawings show how a product fits together

There are a few ways of showing how things fit together —
exploded drawings and sectional drawings are the important ones.

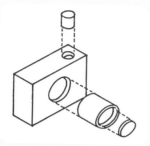

EXPLODED DRAWINGS

1) You draw the product with each separate part of it moved out as if it's been exploded.
2) Each part of the product is drawn in line with the part it is attached to.
3) Dotted lines show where the part has been exploded from.

SECTIONAL DRAWINGS

1) Sectional drawings show additional details.
2) The product is imagined to be cut in half through section X,Y to draw the internal details.

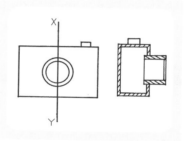

Plan views should be drawn to scale

1) An area can be drawn to scale to show details of where objects are in relation to each other.

2) They're drawn from above.

3) The scale must be shown clearly as a ratio, e.g. 1:2. With a scale of 1:2 the drawing is half the product's actual size. (And of course 1:1 is full size.)

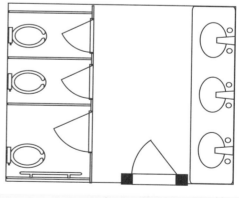

scale 1:100

3rd angle orthographic projection — try saying that 10 times fast...

You need to learn all these details — there's nothing here that you don't need to know. And don't forget to use those British Standards line conventions — they might be a pain, but yer stuck with 'em.

Surfaces, Nets and Boxes

You can make any <u>3-D object</u> by producing a <u>2-D pattern</u> (<u>net</u> or <u>surface development</u>) which you can fold and glue together. You can either do them by hand or you can produce them using <u>CAD/CAM</u>.

You should *know* these *nets* like the *back* of *your hand...*

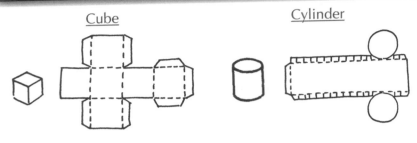

Cube   Cylinder   Triangular-based pyramid

Whenever you're designing a net, <u>remember</u> to:

1) Make it really obvious which lines you're supposed to cut, which will be folded and which areas are to be glued. Use <u>dotted lines</u> for <u>folds</u> and <u>solid lines</u> for <u>cutting</u> and <u>shade</u> areas to be <u>glued</u>.

2) Always include <u>enough tabs</u> to glue your net together.

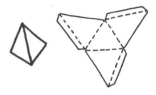

A <u>net</u> is a 2-D plan for making a 3-D object.

Don't forget the *base* — or the *contents* will *fall out*

It's very important that a container has a <u>solid</u> base.

If you want your container to be able to <u>collapse</u> when not in use then you need to include a <u>tuck-in</u> base or <u>automatic</u> base:

1) <u>Tuck-in</u> bases <u>slot into</u> the <u>main part</u> of the box.

2) They often <u>need glue</u> or tape to hold them in place.

1) <u>Automatic</u> bases are <u>formed</u> when the box is <u>constructed</u>.

2) The base is <u>part of</u> the net and <u>no additional glue</u> is needed to ensure it holds firmly.

Use *CAD/CAM* to make sure it's *accurate*

1) Using CAD/CAM (see pages 52 & 81-83) is an ideal way to make sure your net is <u>cut out accurately</u>.

2) You could design your net on a <u>computer</u> using <u>2-D design software</u>.

3) You could then send it to a <u>CAM</u> machine (e.g. a vinyl cutter) which will follow your instructions and <u>cut out</u> or <u>score lines</u> according to your design.

4) You need to tell the CAM machine which lines to cut and which to score. You could do this by <u>colour coding</u> your lines to indicate the <u>depth of cut</u> needed.

Remember — dotted lines for folds, solid lines for cutting...

...and <u>shade in</u> your tabs, then there's no room for confusion. These nets can be quite tricky to start with — you end up chopping off the tabs or making two lids. Keep trying, and don't forget the base.

Graphs and Charts

Any <u>information</u> you collect from a <u>survey</u> or whatever needs to be <u>communicated</u> somehow. Graphs and charts are a <u>nice easy way</u> of making your raw data <u>understandable</u>.

Bar charts use bars to represent information

1) 2-D bar charts can be drawn <u>horizontally</u> or <u>vertically</u>.

2) The information is shown by a series of equally spaced <u>bars</u> of equal width.

3) In this bar chart, different colours are represented by each column. It <u>clearly shows</u> that <u>more people like the colour blue</u> than red or yellow.

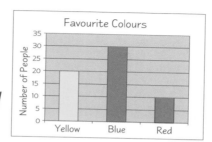

4) Data can also be displayed in <u>3-D bar charts</u>. They're just the same, except the bars look solid.

5) They take the form of simple columns drawn using a particular <u>drawing technique</u>, often <u>oblique</u>.

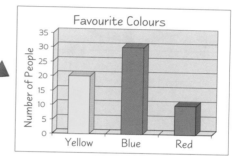

Pictographs are graphs made of pictures

1) Pictographs use <u>symbols</u> or simple <u>pictures</u> to represent information.

2) They make otherwise <u>uninteresting</u> information look <u>more interesting</u>.

3) They're also called <u>pictograms</u> by some people.

Month	Hours of Sunshine
October	☼ ☼ ☼ ☼
November	☼ ☼ ☼
December	☼ ☼
January	☼ ☼ ☼
February	☼ ☼ ☼
March	☼ ☼ ☼ ☼ ☼

☼ represents 2 hours of sunshine per day

The different bars must be equal widths and equal distances apart

This makes it easy for others to see your data clearly. If you think the data is particularly boring, use a pictograph to liven it up a little.

Graphs and Charts

Here's some more types of graphs and charts you can use to communicate your data...

Pie charts show proportions

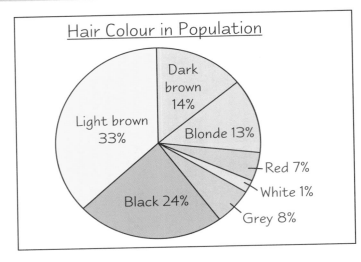

1) Pie charts represent data by <u>dividing</u> a pie or circle into appropriate portions.

2) Each <u>portion</u> of the pie <u>represents</u> a certain category.

3) Pie charts are based on <u>percentages</u>, with the whole pie adding up to 100%.

Line graphs are for continuous data, like time

1) As with bar charts, line graphs show the <u>relationship</u> between <u>two factors</u>, e.g. speed and time.

2) In line graphs you <u>plot</u> the information on the graph and draw a <u>line</u> joining the points.

3) These are pretty handy for <u>spotting trends over time</u>, and also for spotting "<u>blips</u>".

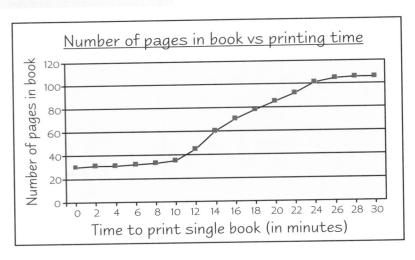

If you've got percentages that add up to 100, use a pie chart

Picking the right type of graph or chart can be a tricky business. Thinking about what kind of information you want to display often helps to choose the right one, e.g. continuous = line graph, not continuous = bar chart, boring = pictograph, proportions = pie chart.

Labels, Icons and Ideograms

Labels and symbols are used on lots of different things to <u>communicate</u> a <u>message</u>. They <u>don't rely on knowing a particular language</u> to understand them.

Enactive labels show how to do something

1) <u>Enactive</u> labels are used to show how to <u>operate</u> a product.
2) They are usually <u>universally recognised</u> and don't include words.
3) Examples of enactive labels are the control buttons on a stereo:

Iconic labels — simple and easily recognised

1) Examples of <u>iconic</u> labels appear on your <u>computer</u> screen as <u>shortcuts</u> to software, files or program tools.
2) Icons that identify <u>functions</u> (e.g. the text tool) are similar in <u>all</u> software packages, to help a user to <u>quickly learn</u> how to use <u>new software</u>.
3) Icons are usually <u>little</u>, and <u>immediately</u> recognisable to the user.

And don't forget good old sportswear labelling — people will spend a lot of money just to have that icon stuck on their chest.

Ideograms use pictures to represent ideas

1) <u>Ideograms</u> (<u>pictograms</u>) can be <u>substituted</u> for writing — they're kind of a <u>universal language</u>.
2) They're <u>images</u> that are easily and immediately <u>identifiable</u>.
3) You'll have seen plenty of ideograms in <u>everyday life</u> — e.g. if you go on holiday, you might see a <u>sign</u> with an aeroplane to identify an airport, or one with a telephone receiver pointing to a payphone.

Non-standard symbols can be created

1) If a label doesn't already exist for an object, you can <u>create</u> one.
2) These <u>rules</u> are useful when designing your own label or icon:

> 1) Try not to use any <u>words</u>, so it can be used in any country.
> 2) Make sure the symbol's <u>relevant</u> to the object you're labelling.
> 3) Make sure the symbol is able to be <u>reproduced</u> if it's going to be used on a number of items.
> 4) Keep it <u>simple</u>.
> 5) Make sure it's an appropriate <u>colour</u>.

In most cases people don't consciously think about the colour — they might just instinctively associate a particular colour with a feeling — like red for danger.

There are some standard colouring conventions that it's worth considering — such as:

1) <u>Red</u> for <u>STOP or warning</u>
2) <u>Green</u> for <u>GO or OK</u> or for something <u>environmentally friendly</u> or <u>vegetarian</u>

Symbols are used as a universal language

Words would never work if you wanted everyone in the world to understand. Whereas a picture like this on a gate is clearly telling you not to go in there or you'll die.

Branding

You should be really familiar with this subject — branding is all around you everyday...

Graphics are everywhere — promoting **brands**

Graphics (i.e. <u>words</u>, <u>pictures</u> and <u>symbols</u>) are applied to a wide <u>range</u> of <u>products</u> in lots of different situations. On the average high street you can see loads of examples of logos, trademarks, corporate imagery and visual advertising, etc.

You'll see them on:
1) <u>shopfronts</u> and <u>shop signs</u>,
2) <u>delivery vehicles</u>,
3) <u>shopping bags</u>,
4) confectionery and fast-food <u>packaging</u>,
5) workers' <u>equipment</u> and <u>uniforms</u>,
6) <u>stationery</u>,
7) <u>static advertisements</u> e.g. billboards,
8) <u>mobile advertisements</u> e.g. on buses,
9) <u>branded clothing</u> worn by members of the public.

Strong **corporate identity** means good **brand recognition**

1) Many companies have a <u>corporate look</u> or <u>identity</u> — they apply their <u>logo</u> and <u>colour scheme</u> to <u>all printed material</u> (e.g. business cards, letterheads and compliments slips) — as well as their products, packaging, uniforms and transport.

2) Companies like Body Shop, MacDonald's and Nike have <u>very strong corporate identities</u>. Most people can recognise each company from its colours or logo alone, without the need for words. This is great for the company.

3) The most successful corporate images/colours are those which are <u>flexible</u> enough to be applied to <u>different surfaces</u> whilst still retaining their impact and recognisability.

Companies like to brand their products

With branding graphics, the simple, unfussy designs are most effective. Remember, good brand graphics need to be versatile. For example, you might need transfers, stickers, embroidered patches, and all sorts of things to get your design onto all the necessary surfaces.

Flow Charts and Sequential Illustrations

Flow charts show the stages of an operation clearly by breaking them down into little chunks.

A flow chart shows events in the order they happen

1) A flow chart is a diagram which shows a number of events in the order that they take place.

2) Each event has a symbol (a shaped box).

3) Different symbols show different types of event, e.g. decisions or operations.

4) Inside each symbol is something that explains what is happening at that stage. It could be a word, a few words, a photograph or a drawing.

Flow charts use standard symbols

1) At the beginning or the end of a flow chart there is always a sausage shape.

2) Operations or processes are represented by rectangles.

3) Questions or decisions are represented by rhombuses (diamond shapes).

4) Arrows are drawn between each event to show the flow and the direction of the flow.

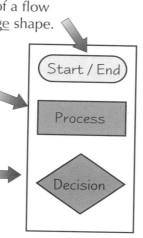

Flow chart for crossing a road:

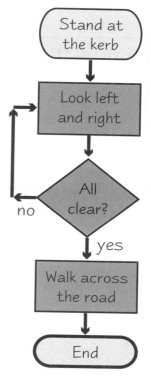

You can also use sequential illustrations

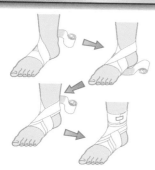

1) Instead of producing a flow chart, you can use a series of illustrations to show how to do something.

2) You'll see examples of this when you buy flat-pack furniture — it comes with simple instructions that show how to build it.

3) These instructions use pictures and very few words so that everybody should be able to follow them.

Each event in a flow chart has a symbol

You need to know the symbols and what they mean — so you're just gonna have to learn them. Once you know them you can make brilliant flow-charts — just what you always wanted.

Warm-up and Worked Exam Questions

Well done, only these few pages of questions and then you're half way through your graphic products revision. Use the warm-up questions to check you remember the basic facts from this section.

Warm-up Questions

1) Why are symbols or simple pictures sometimes used to represent information on a graph?
2) What name do we give to a graph that uses symbols or pictures instead of numbers?
3) What is the purpose of enactive labels?
4) What does this sign mean?

5) Give two different uses of a flow chart?

Exam questions don't vary that wildly and the basic format is the same. So once you've been through this worked example and done the questions after it, you'll be a good distance along the right track.

Worked Exam Questions

1   The picture below shows the end view of a matchbox.

Using the single point perspective technique and the vanishing point provided, adapt the picture into a correctly proportioned 3-D view of a matchbox.

Here you have to make sure that the sketch uses single point perspective, AND that it looks correctly proportioned, to get both marks.

Vanishing point

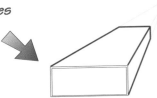

(2 marks)

2   Have a look at the pie chart below.

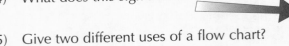

Key
A = 10 votes
B
C

a)   How many votes are represented by sections B and C respectively?

B is 6 votes. C is 4 votes.

(2 marks)

b)   A survey shows the following information about telephone type preferences. 20 people prefer flip phones, 15 people prefer slide-apart phones, and 5 people prefer rotate-apart phones.

On the circle below draw an approximate pie chart showing these telephone type preferences:

If you have to draw a graph or a pie chart, remember to include labels or a key.

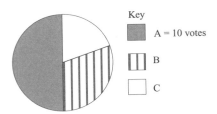

Key
Flip phones
Rotate-apart phones
Slide-apart phones

(6 marks)

Exam Questions

3   A new company called PC Zone want a logo/brand mark designed.

   a)   Using the letters PCZ, develop one logo suitable for PC Zone's letter headed paper. Draw it in the box below.

(2 marks)

   b)   Name four places where you would expect to find the brand mark of a medium sized company.

....

....

....

....

(4 marks)

   c)   Give two reasons why simple images for logos and brand marks more suitable than complex images?

....

....

(2 marks)

4   The logo is to be fixed to the inside of a shop window. PC Zone want the sign to be made from vinyl.

   a)   How can the logo be drawn, so that the sticky side of the vinyl faces the glass, and not the inside of the shop?

....

....

(2 marks)

   b)   What type of CAM equipment should be used to cut out the design?

....

(2 marks)

Revision Summary for Section Four

This section is packed with stuff to learn. You should find the next few questions easy, so have a go and see how you get on. If you get any wrong have a quick look back and try again. And repeat this process until you get every single one right.

1) Name two 3-D drawing techniques.

2) In perspective drawing, what is a vanishing point?

3) In perspective drawing, what do we mean by the horizon line?

4) When should you use each type of perspective drawing?

5) What angle is an object drawn at in an isometric drawing?

6) What is the symbol for 3rd angle orthographic projection?

7) What three views are drawn when completing a 3rd angle orthographic projection of an object?

8) Draw an exploded drawing of a toy car.

9) Why might you draw a sectional drawing of an object?

10) How can you make a 3-D object using a sheet of cardboard?

11) What do you need to consider when designing a net?

12) What is an automatic base?

13) How could you use CAD/CAM to cut out your shape net?

14) What is a bar chart? What is a 3-D bar chart?

15) What is the difference between a bar chart and a pictograph? Why might you draw a pictograph rather than a bar chart?

16) What is a pie chart? What percentage does a full pie chart add up to?

17) What is an enactive label? Draw the enactive labels that you'd expect to find on a stereo.

18) Why are ideograms/pictograms more suitable for use around the world than labels containing words or numbers?

19) Write down five rules to remember when designing your own non-standard symbol.

20) How could colour be used in designing labels?

21) On the average high street, where might you find examples of logos and branding?

22) What is a flow chart? How are they used to show clearly a process from start to finish?

23) What are the correct symbols for the beginning/end, processes and decisions on flow charts?

24) Produce some assembly instructions for assembling a flat-pack unit with three shelves that fix together with screws onto two outside panels, as shown to the right.

Why People Buy a Product

If you know what makes people buy things, it becomes <u>easier</u> to design stuff they'll want. So for a designer, finding out this information is dead important.

Good *design* and good *manufacture* are *different* things

A well-designed product:
- has the potential to carry out its <u>function</u> really well — because the <u>thinking</u> that's gone into the design is good,
- <u>looks</u> good and attracts consumers.

A well-manufactured product:
- has been <u>made</u> to a <u>good standard</u> — things like the finish, folds, colour and material are all satisfactory,
- is <u>accurate</u> to the original design.

Customers *choose* products for *different reasons*

Not everyone buys a product for the same reasons. People might buy something because of:

1) <u>Cost</u> — Customers might think the product is good <u>value for money</u>.
2) <u>Brand loyalty</u> — Customers might be <u>loyal</u> to a company after finding previous goods to be good quality.
3) <u>Aesthetic appeal</u> — Customers might like the <u>look</u> and <u>design</u> of the product.
4) <u>Advertising</u> — This raises <u>product awareness</u>, and can make customers more likely to buy a product.
5) <u>Fashion</u> — Some customers will be more likely to buy something they think is <u>up to date</u> and <u>trendy</u>.

Manufacturers *survey* current *market trends*

It's important for manufacturers to know what <u>consumers think</u> of their product. In order to improve their product they have to keep up with <u>current trends</u> in the market. They have to know:

- What colours, materials and styles are <u>fashionable</u>.
- If consumers like the <u>design</u> and <u>quality</u> of their product.
- If consumers like their <u>advertising</u>.
- How much <u>money</u> consumers are willing to pay for the product.

See page 73 for more on how manufacturers can find this stuff out.

Manufacturers also need certain things from a *product*

<u>Manufacturers</u> will have opinions on what makes a 'good' product. Manufacturers often work out a set of <u>criteria</u> stating what they want from a new product. They might require that:

1) The time taken to manufacture and assemble the different parts of the product is reasonably fast.
2) The materials and equipment used to manufacture the product are easy to obtain and cost-effective.
3) The product meets a need — consumers will find it useful.
4) The product carries out its function well — it has been designed and manufactured to a high standard.
5) The product looks good and will be attractive to consumers.

Why buy it? Because it's there...

People are more likely to buy things they want — that's no surprise. But being able to decide <u>what</u> consumers want and <u>why</u> can be worth more money than winning the lottery. So it's important.

Evaluation

Even <u>after</u> a product's been manufactured, the design process doesn't really <u>stop</u>.
In industry, the process of evaluation and improvement is <u>ongoing</u>.

The **finished product** needs to be evaluated

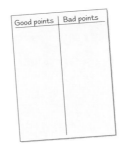

Good points	Bad points

1) Once a product has been finished, its <u>strengths</u>
and <u>weaknesses</u> need to be assessed.

2) This is so that <u>lessons</u> can be learnt for <u>future</u> products.
For example, are any <u>safety modifications</u> necessary, or
could any <u>improvements</u> be made?

3) Similarly, it's important to record any <u>problems</u> that were encountered and
how they were <u>overcome</u>. This goes for both the <u>design</u> and <u>manufacturing</u>
stages. It might help avoid similar problems next time.

4) It's important to get <u>other people's opinions</u> as well
when it comes to evaluating a product — ask <u>potential</u>
<u>users</u> and <u>experts</u> who have designed this kind of
product before (see next page for more on this).

Quality Control

Part of the ongoing evaluation process is to monitor quality all the time the product is
being manufactured. <u>Checks</u> need to be made at various stages of the manufacturing
process to make sure the product is being produced to the <u>highest</u> possible <u>standard</u>.

Records of everything are kept from the **very start**

1) From the very first moment of the design process,
<u>records</u> of <u>ideas</u>, <u>prototypes</u>, <u>experiments</u>, etc. are kept.

2) These records can be in the form of <u>written notes</u>, <u>data</u> from
experiments, <u>videos</u> of prototypes being tested, and so on.

3) This makes it easy to see <u>why</u> certain ideas were <u>dropped</u> and why others were <u>persevered</u> with.

4) It might sometimes be necessary to go back to an earlier idea,
and this is made much <u>easier</u> if proper records have been kept.

Why evaluations are **important**

1) Designers are always looking at ways to
<u>improve</u> their designs.

2) Companies employ designers to make use
of the <u>latest innovations</u> in technology.

3) If designers were always <u>happy</u> with how
things were, we wouldn't have seen
the innovations in technology that we
all take for granted.

Unless designers can be <u>critical</u> of
their designs in a constructive way:

1) Their designs would <u>never improve</u>.

2) Products would <u>fail to keep up</u> with
the latest trends and fashions.

Evaluating is a good way to figure out how to improve your product

Don't underestimate how important an evaluation of a finished product is. If you don't
improve upon your product, someone else will. If nobody evaluated their products and
made them better we would all still be watching black and white TV and wearing shell suits.

Evaluation

There are various ways to evaluate a product. The designers have a big role to play in any evaluation, but so do the people who will actually use the product.

Comment on the **success** of your final design

The most obvious way to evaluate a finished product is to compare it against its original design specification. But there are other measures of success as well, such as:

1) Function — How well does the final design meet the intended task — does it work?
2) Timescale — Did you complete the task on time?
   Did some things take more/less time to complete than others?
3) Safety — Is the design safe? Were all safety precautions taken during making?
4) Cost — Has the design been made within the original budget?
5) Ergonomics — Is the design practical — could the majority of people use it?
6) Materials — Were the materials used the right ones to use?
   If not, suggest what materials could have been used and why.
7) Aesthetics — Comment on the visual success of the product.
   Mention its colour, shape, layout, visual impact, size (and you could also mention its texture and feel while you're doing this kind of thing).
8) Environmental — Did you make good use of materials and resources?
   Could there have been less waste generated?

Talk to your **target audience**

It's also important to ask the intended users of a product what they think of it. Things to find out might include:

1) Is the product easy to use?
2) Is it well made?
3) Is it easy to maintain?
4) Does it look attractive?

Get opinions using **questionnaires** and **focus groups**

Manufacturers can get information from consumers in different ways, for example:

QUESTIONNAIRES These ask a series of questions about consumer habits and preferences. A large number and variety of people can be targeted with a questionnaire.

FOCUS GROUPS In these a small group of consumers are encouraged to discuss their opinions about the product in detail.

You might think your product is great... but do other people?

Questionnaires and focus groups — what a barrel of laughs. But they are important. Questionnaires are great for collecting data about how many people think this or that, whereas focus groups are better for finding out why they think as they do.

Moral and Cultural Issues

It's no good designing the best pair of pants ever if no one will wear them because the design is offensive in some way. You need to be sensitive and avoid offending people unnecessarily.

Designs must be *socially* and *environmentally responsible*

When you're selecting materials, components and manufacturing processes, you need to consider:

1) Whether using the product might harm people or the environment (this includes finding out whether any materials used, including paints and varnishes, are toxic).

2) Whether the manufacture of the product harms people, e.g. through dangerous working conditions for manufacturing workers, or because components are produced using child labour.

3) Whether the manufacture of the product harms the environment, e.g. consider how much waste material will be produced, and how it's going to be disposed of.

4) Whether recycled materials could be used to manufacture the product or its packaging.

5) Whether biodegradable or recyclable materials could be used (especially if the product's designed to be thrown away after use).

Be *aware* of the *feelings* of others

You'll need to exercise a little sensitivity when you're designing stuff...

1) Designers need to be sensitive to the feelings of different groups in society.

2) Make sure that your design does not put off, insult or offend people for political, religious, gender or cultural reasons.

3) Certain symbols are almost certain to offend some people no matter how they're used, e.g. a swastika.

4) Other symbolism will offend people if they believe it's been misused or abused. This is especially true for religious symbols.

5) But it's not only abuse of religious symbols which can cause offence. Other images, colours and styles can easily put people from certain cultures off a product.

6) Some things might not be obvious at all — for instance, certain colours are seen as good or bad luck in some cultures.

This sort of thing might have appeared in the 1920s...

...but you wouldn't get away with it today.

7) More obvious examples include nudity and violence. Although images containing nudity or violence won't offend everyone, it's very possible that you will end up offending some people.

8) It's impossible to list everything that could cause offence. You just have to try and put yourself in other people's shoes, and use a little imagination to guess how they might feel when they see your design.

Watch what you're saying — better sensitive than sorry...

Designers have got to think about this sort of stuff nowadays, since consumers pay more attention to the way products have been made. It's a good thing, since it eases environmental problems — and means people are less likely to be exploited by being paid poor wages, etc.

Environmental Issues

We live in a consumer culture where everyone wants to <u>own</u> and <u>upgrade</u> their possessions. This is all well and good, but the consequences for the <u>environment</u> can be pretty severe.

Manufacturing products causes **environmental problems**

1) The <u>rainforests</u> are a prime example of a <u>threatened resource</u>. They produce valuable and exotic <u>hardwoods</u> which are (mostly) <u>not being replaced</u>. There are <u>sustainable</u> hardwood plantations in some countries, but it <u>costs money</u> to organise them and check that they're all above board.

2) <u>Softwoods</u> (which can regenerate themselves in a person's lifetime) are a <u>greener choice</u>, as are <u>recycled</u> materials that <u>use waste wood</u>, e.g. chipboard.

3) However, <u>single-species plantations</u> aren't ideal — they're unable to <u>support</u> many other animal and plant species, leading to a reduction in <u>biodiversity</u>.

4) It isn't just trees that we need to worry about, however. <u>Metal ores</u> are taken from the Earth's crust, and there's only a <u>limited amount</u> of each ore.

5) Also, most <u>plastics</u> come from <u>oil</u>. Oil is drilled from the Earth's crust and there's only a limited amount down there, so it will eventually <u>run out</u>.

Throwing **away** old products causes **pollution**

At the end of its life, an old product needs to be <u>disposed of</u> to make way for a shiny new one.

- Most waste goes into <u>landfill</u>. Some chemicals used in products cause <u>serious problems</u> when they get into watercourses or into the soil.

- There are <u>laws</u> about what can be dumped into landfill sites and what has to be <u>recycled</u> or <u>specially treated</u> to make it <u>safe</u>.

<u>Packaging</u> (see page 99) contributes to the problem of waste. Designers need to assess <u>how much</u> packaging is actually <u>needed</u> for a product, and how it will be <u>disposed of</u> or <u>recycled</u>.

Damage can be caused by product manufacture and disposal

It's not just throwing away old products that damages the environment — extracting the raw materials to manufacture products often uses harmful processes, e.g. mining, oil drilling and logging.

Environmental Issues

If you're going to manufacture something you can at least make it recyclable so it doesn't damage the environment too much...

Recycling can help

1) Reusing or recycling products can save <u>money</u> and <u>energy</u>, and help protect the <u>environment</u>.

2) <u>Glass</u> is the most widely used recycled material, but there are plenty of others, e.g. paper, aluminium and some plastics.

3) Some containers (like those for washing-up liquid, fabric conditioners, etc.) are <u>refillable</u>. <u>Refilling</u> used containers is even <u>better</u> than recycling them.

4) The 'Möbius Loop' means that the product can be <u>recycled</u>, or that it contains some recyclable material. (The three arrows symbolise the 3 Rs — see page 99.)

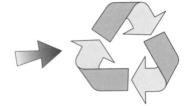

5) The '<u>Green Dot</u>' (<u>der Grüne Punkt</u>) shows that the packaging supplier has <u>contributed</u> to the <u>cost</u> of <u>recycling</u> or <u>recovering</u> the material used — it doesn't necessarily mean that the packaging is recyclable.

Paper that's been printed on can be recycled, but the ink content means recycled paper is <u>darker</u> in colour or has a <u>speckled</u> appearance. (It wouldn't be environmentally friendly to <u>bleach</u> it white again.)

Recycling isn't all plain sailing — it can be <u>more expensive</u> to <u>recycle old</u> materials than to <u>use new ones</u>. Also, <u>environmentally unfriendly by-products</u> can be produced in the recycling process, which sort of defeats the point a bit.

Try to recycle what you can
In the past, not as many people either knew or cared about the damage that industry and modern living does to the environment. Now we're better informed and more aware — and we're finding that there are loads of things we can do to reduce the effects of our consumer culture.

Legal Issues

You need to be aware of the different rules and regulations regarding design — if you don't know about these you could find yourself in trouble...

Trademarks and patents stop people stealing ideas

1) The aim of using trademarks is to stop people from selling <u>copies</u> of <u>well-known brands</u>.

2) Individuals or companies can register <u>trademarks</u> with the <u>Patent Office</u>. Trademarks are <u>distinctive</u> logos, words or pictures that identify a particular company or product. If someone else then uses your trademark (or something <u>similar</u>), you can <u>sue</u> them.

3) <u>Patents</u> are granted when something new has been <u>invented</u>. They allow the inventor (for a <u>limited time</u>) to stop others from making, using or selling the invention <u>without permission</u>.

4) For a patent to be granted, the invention must involve an '<u>inventive step</u>' (you won't get a patent for something that's dead obvious), and must be capable of '<u>industrial application</u>' (so you won't get a patent for a nice painting you've done).

Other legislation protects consumers and workers

1) <u>The Trade Descriptions Act</u> (1968) applies to all goods. If you're going to be selling anything, you have to be truthful in the way you describe it. This will be important when it comes to making packaging for your product, or advertising it.

2) <u>COSHH</u> stands for the <u>Containment of Substances Hazardous to Health</u>. The COSHH regulations were introduced in 1988 to protect people from the effects of <u>hazardous substances</u>, <u>materials</u> and <u>processes</u>.

Products can be labelled if they meet certain standards

These standards are usually concerned with <u>safety</u>, <u>quality</u> or <u>design</u>.

1) There are various <u>institutes</u> that set <u>standards</u> for certain types of product.

2) Products that meet these standards can usually be <u>labelled</u> to show this (see page 78).

3) It can be <u>important</u> for a manufacturer's products to meet these standards, as many <u>consumers</u> are more willing to buy '<u>approved</u>' products.

4) The <u>British Standards Institute (BSI)</u> is one example of this kind of standards institute. Products that meet its standards may display its 'Kitemark'.

5) The <u>International Standards Organisation</u> (<u>ISO</u>) also issues <u>certificates</u> to organisations that meet international standards of quality.

6) And if certain products are going to be sold within the <u>European Union</u> (<u>EU</u>), then they have to be '<u>CE marked</u>'. The CE mark shows that the product has met <u>standards</u> set by the EU.

Other examples of these awarding bodies include:	• the <u>British Electrotechnical Approvals Board</u> (BEAB), • the <u>British Toy and Hobby Manufacturers' Association</u> (BTMA).

Patents stop other people copying your ideas... and vice versa

If you have a brilliant idea that you think is going to make your fortune, then my advice would be to get a patent. That way, you can be sure that you'll get the money that your invention surely deserves. And if your invention meets all the relevant standards, then so much the better.

Labels

Manufacturers are legally obliged to put certain information on packaging, and they're responsible for making sure that it's all true. Anyway, I'll let you get on with the page now...

Manufacturers must **label** their products **carefully**

There are various laws in the UK which describe what information labels on products must give, and protect consumers against dishonest labelling. For example:

1) Trade Descriptions Act (1968) — see page 77.
2) Food Labelling Regulations (1996) — these state what information must be on food packaging.
3) Food Safety Act (1990) — this says that food must be correctly described.

Labels can give information about **safety**

1) Certain institutes allow manufacturers to label their products with special labels if certain standards have been met (see page 77).
2) Labels also help consumers use and maintain a product.
3) They can give useful safety instructions, such as, *"This way up"*, *"Ensure catch is fully locked before use"* or *"Danger — this part gets hot during use"*.
4) Or they can give maintenance instructions such as, *"Clean with warm water only"*, *"Do not use abrasives"*, *"Oil frequently"* or *"Do not immerse in water"*.

Food labels have to tell you **certain information**

The Food Labelling Regulations state that labels on processed foods must give this information:

1) The name of the product and what it is.
2) What ingredients the product contains, in descending order of weight — preservatives, colourants, emulsifiers and other additives must also be listed (but not flavourings).
3) The name and address of the manufacturer, as well as the country of origin of the ingredients (if from a single country).
4) How the product should be stored.
5) The weight or volume of the product.
6) A best-before or use-by date.
7) Instructions for preparation and cooking (if necessary).
8) Whether a product contains genetically modified ingredients (if greater than 1%).

Nutritional information sometimes has to be **included**

NUTRITIONAL INFORMATION		
	per 100g	per 55g serving
Energy	2180kJ/525 kcal	1199kJ/289 kcal
Protein	6.5g	3.6g
Carbohydrate	50.0g	27.5g
of which sugars	2.0g	1.1g
Fat	33.0g	18.2g
of which saturates	15.0g	8.3g
Sodium	0.7g	0.4g
Fibre	4.0g	2.2g

- If a special nutritional claim has been made (e.g. 'low sugar') then products must, by law, show the nutritional information.
- This information is often shown in the form of a table.
- It usually shows energy values, protein, carbohydrate, fat, fibre and sodium per 100g and per portion.

Learn what information manufacturers have to put on labels

Although reading this page and learning what's on it may make you want to go to sleep, worry not. It's only a page long and once you've learnt it all you can go and take a well-deserved 5-minute break. It's important stuff, so learn it well.

Warm-up and Worked Exam Questions

Here's a well deserved mid-section break for you. Use the warm-up questions to check what you've learnt so far, make sure you look up anything you're unsure about.

Warm-up Questions

1) What moral or ethical reason is there to recycle plastic?
2) What is the name of the organisation represented by this symbol?

3) Give three examples of information that must be included on food packaging/labels.
4) Why do manufacturers want to know what customers think about their products, after they have been sold and used?
5) What is the purpose of a patent?

Just this set of pesky practice questions stand between you and the rest of the section, so pens at the ready and get to it.

Worked Exam Questions

1   a)   Give two problems caused by waste in landfill sites.

Water courses can be contaminated by leaking chemicals from waste.

They can produce explosive methane gas.

(2 marks)

b)   Name one way of dealing with waste, other than dumping it in landfill sites.

It can be recycled.

(1 mark)

c)   Name two ways in which graphic designers can encourage users to dispose of packaging waste in an environmentally friendly way.

They could design products and packaging that have recycle symbols

and information, and they could also use the litter disposal symbol.

(2 marks)

2   Why should manufacturers consider the reaction of people from different cultures to their products and packaging?

a)   Give one reason based on business sense.

People could have different tastes they would not buy the product.

Remember, people can be offended by images, phrases, colours and styles. This could be because of political, religious, gender or cultural reasons.

(1 mark)

b)   Give one reason based on social or cultural issues.

People might be offended by words or pictures on the product.

(1 mark)

Exam Questions

3   The Rapid Radio Company are manufacturers of hand held electronic products. They have
     decided to enter the personal music player market. They want to know what young people
     think about personal music players that are already on the market.

a)   Name three areas of research that manufacturers could investigate before they write
     their design brief.

     ....

     ....

     ....

                                                                                          (3 marks)

b)   The Rapid Radio Company also have certain manufacturing priorities. List three
     important considerations they should make about the way they organise and
     manufacture a new product.

     ....

     ....

     ....

                                                                                          (3 marks)

4   In order to attract and retain a good workforce, the Rapid Radio Company are looking for
     ways to take care of their workers.

     Using each of the three headings below, write a question that will help them to analyse
     opportunities for improvement in their factory.

a)   Safety: for the workers during manufacture.

     ....

                                                                                          (1 mark)

b)   Ergonomics: making the work easier or more interesting for workers.

     ....

                                                                                          (1 mark)

c)   Environmental: from the workers' point of view.

     ....

                                                                                          (1 mark)

CAD — Computer-Aided Design

CAD is used in the design of many everyday products — from seatbelts through to aeroplanes.

Computer-Aided Design (CAD) is used for plans and models

CAD is design using computer drawing and modelling packages such as Pro/DESKTOP and Techsoft 2D. They are used by architects, designers and engineers to produce detailed plans, drawings and product simulations. CAD is fast becoming a major part of D&T project work.

Learn these advantages of CAD

1) Designs can be re-sized (up or down) easily.

2) Designs can be modified quickly and easily without the need for the whole drawing to be done again.

3) It can save costly office space as drawings are stored on hard drives and compact disks instead of bulky plan chests.

4) It can save time and labour and is therefore cost-effective.

5) Designing using CAD can be done on a laptop computer — at home, on the train, etc.

This is "Techsoft Design Tools — 2D design".

6) Designs can be sent directly and instantly to a client or manufacturer by ISDN or e-mail.

7) Designs and drawings can be in 3-D as well as 2-D and can be viewed from any angle. Also, scales of components in relation to each other can be worked out.

8) Objects drawn with CAD packages can be presented as wireframe models or solid models. They can even be rendered to look like plastic or glass, etc. for customer presentations and 'virtual prototyping'.

9) CAD can be used to create tests and simulations of how a product or material will perform in a given situation without the need to build expensive testing rigs or full-scale prototypes.

CAD has disadvantages too

1) The initial outlay on software and hardware is high.

2) Expensive and lengthy training is required for best results. Not just any random person off the street can walk into a studio and start designing stuff.

3) Viruses, corrupt files and power cuts can interrupt and destroy work, just like with all IT-based work.

4) Traditional skills and processes may become obsolete, and jobs may be lost.

CAD makes designing loads easier than it used to be

When using a CAD package, save your work regularly in case of power loss or crashing computers. Basic computer common sense, but it's easy to forget once you're well stuck in.

CAM — Computer-Aided Manufacture

CAD is clever, but CAM is really clever. That's what I reckon, anyway.
This is all dead important in industry, and is becoming more important in D&T projects as well.

Computer-Aided Manufacture (CAM) is used for making products

Computer-Aided Manufacture is the process of manufacturing goods using information received from a CAD package.

1) Data from CAD software is downloaded into the control unit of a manufacturing machine.

2) Components and products are then made on machines (such as milling machines) that are controlled and operated by computers rather than by a person.

3) Popular makes of CAM machines used in schools include: Boxford, Denford, Unimatics and Roland.

Learn the advantages of CAM

1) Minor (or major) modifications can easily be made without expensive retooling costs.

2) Repeat jobs can be quickly downloaded and set up — making small batch-produced items cost-effective and feasible.

3) It can save time and labour and reduce errors — again making it more cost-effective.

4) It allows the manufacture of products in situations which may be harmful to humans.

5) Machines can do more complex jobs more accurately and in less time.

6) Machines do not need to rest, so productivity is increased.

But there are some disadvantages too

They're pretty much the same as the disadvantages of CAD on the previous page, but they're really important to learn, so here they are again:

1) The computer equipment is expensive.

2) You need loads of training to use it — this takes time and money.

3) There are also the usual problems that you get with using computers, like viruses and crashes.

4) People who are skilled in using traditional methods may lose their jobs.

It all comes down to man versus machine, really.

CAM makes continuous production possible

This computer-controlled stuff is really quite clever. Learn all the numbered points then write a mini essay explaining the advantages and disadvantages of CAM — it'll really help you remember the facts.

CAM — Computer-Aided Manufacture

You need to learn about the machines that CAM uses — so here they are...

CAM uses *Computer Numerically Controlled (CNC)* machines

1) The machines used in the CAM process are <u>Computer Numerically Controlled</u>.

2) This means the CAD/CAM program works out the necessary <u>movements</u> of the <u>tool head</u> and <u>sends the data</u> to the machine in the form of numbers. The machine's <u>onboard processor</u> interprets the numbers and controls the movement of the tool head.

3) Machines which can be controlled in this way include <u>lathes</u>, <u>milling</u> machines, <u>drilling</u> machines and <u>flame cutters</u>.

The CAMM1 — a CNC cutter and plotter.

There are loads of *advantages* of CNC

1) <u>Less cost</u> due to less need for separate specialised machine tools for each product.

2) <u>Less</u> chance of human <u>error</u>.

3) The product can <u>easily</u> and quickly be <u>changed</u> without expensive retooling.

A CNC milling machine.

There are also some *disadvantages*

1) <u>High initial cost</u> of the machines.

2) <u>High cost of training</u> programmers and operators.

3) Fast <u>special purpose machines</u> are <u>cheaper</u> than CNC machines for large-scale production runs.

CNCs have brains.... well, onboard processors...

Now that people can use CAD/CAM to design things really quickly, it means that they can let their imaginations run wild. There's nothing to lose by trying out lots of different designs on-screen.

DTP

DTP stands for <u>Desktop Publishing</u>. It's a way of laying out a publication using a computer, rather than doing it all by hand, (see page 38 for more info). It produces very professional looking pages.

There are **loads of reasons** for using **DTP**

1) It saves <u>time</u> and <u>money</u>, since designers can see exactly what a layout will look like before spending money making a colour printed proof.

2) Text and graphics can be <u>arranged</u> <u>anywhere</u> on the page.

3) Designers can <u>experiment</u> more and create more <u>complex</u> designs.

4) Fonts can be easily <u>resized</u> on screen.

5) Scanned <u>images</u> can be <u>imported</u> and incorporated into a design.

6) Designs can be <u>stored</u>, <u>edited</u> and <u>updated</u>.

7) Designs can go <u>directly to press</u> digitally, without loss of quality.

8) Photographs and drawings can be <u>sized</u> and <u>cropped</u> — giving the designer more <u>flexibility</u>.

<u>Microsoft</u>® <u>Publisher</u>, <u>QuarkXpress</u>®, <u>Adobe</u>® <u>InDesign</u>® and <u>Adobe</u>® <u>Pagemaker</u>® are examples of DTP programs.

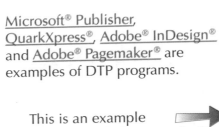

This is an example of what Adobe® Pagemaker® looks like.

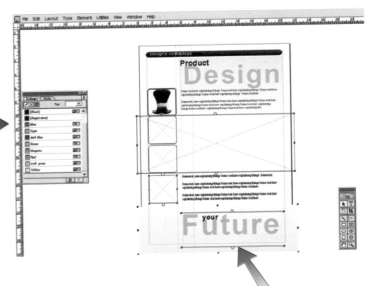

This is a single frame containing the text 'your future'.

DTP software is usually **frame based**

1) Frame-based software means that information is put on pages in <u>blocks</u> (called <u>frames</u>).

2) Frames can be <u>moved</u> or <u>resized</u>. This means it is very <u>easy to</u> <u>edit</u> a DTP document by moving pictures or blocks of text around. Frames can also be moved from page to page.

DTP is really easy and it makes professional looking pages

If you want to impress everyone with your work then try using some DTP software to make it look good. Place your images and text in separate frames — that way you can move it around really easily.

Photo-Editing Software

Graphics can make a printed page <u>look nice</u>, and they can also help you get your point across.

Graphics spice up a page

It's all very well wanting <u>graphics</u> on your page, but you have to <u>input</u> the <u>image</u> into the computer first.

These are the three main ways to input an image:

(1) Use a scanner

(2) Use a digital camera

(3) Use clipart

Once your image is in the computer, you might want to change it a bit...

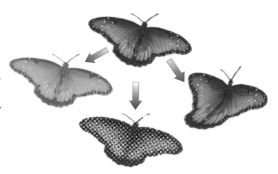

1) <u>Adobe® Photoshop®</u> and <u>Corel Photo-paint®</u> are two examples of photo-editing software — they can be used to <u>retouch</u> and <u>manipulate</u> digital images.

2) Images are stored as thousands of dots called <u>pixels</u>. If you zoom in close enough, you can see the individual pixels.

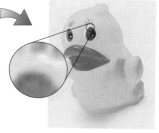

3) Information about the colour of each <u>individual</u> pixel has to be stored, so this kind of image can take up <u>lots of memory</u>.

4) Information on computer screens is displayed using just <u>red</u>, <u>green</u> and <u>blue</u> — <u>RGB</u>. By combining these three colours, every other colour can be displayed. (This is also how a TV works.)

5) However, images are usually converted to <u>cyan</u>, <u>magenta</u>, <u>yellow</u>, and <u>black</u> (<u>CMYK</u>) for printing (see p49). Each of these colours is printed on paper separately, with the black being applied last.

'K' stands for 'key', but it means 'black'.

You could see what your product looks like in a different colour...

Designers retouch photographs to make things look as perfect as possible — so you'll never see a photograph of a model in a magazine with a big spot. It's good to experiment with this kind of software — you'll find you can create loads of different visual effects once you get the hang of it.

ICT in Industry

Computers are everywhere these days... the design and manufacturing industry use them a lot.

Increased use of ICT has good and bad effects

ICT is used more and more in offices, schools, homes, shops, banks... well, pretty much everywhere. People at work, and particularly those in office jobs, have to spend more and more time using computers. This has pros and cons:

PROS

1) Employers benefit because computers can increase the amount of work done. This makes businesses more productive, and so more competitive.
2) Workers benefit if computers can do boring, repetitive tasks and leave them to do the interesting jobs.
3) Transferring data electronically is quick and convenient.
4) The Internet is really useful as a research tool.

CONS

1) It's expensive to keep investing in the latest and most efficient technology, and it takes time and money to retrain staff.
2) There may be job losses as computers replace people for some tasks, such as car assembly.
3) Continued use of computers can cause health problems, e.g. repetitive strain injury (RSI).

The electronic transfer of data is useful for industry

The electronic transfer of data is dead useful in industry.

1) It means that design work and manufacturing work can be done in separate locations. A designer's work can be electronically transferred to the manufacturing site.
2) Electronic Data Interchange (EDI) is the direct transfer of information from one computer system to another, usually via the telephone network.
3) E-mail can be used to quickly transfer written information between different locations.
4) Teleconferencing allows meetings between workers in different locations. It uses a camera connected to a computer which is connected to the telephone network or Internet. Voices and moving images are relayed in real time.

The World Wide Web can be used as a research tool

There's a huge amount of information on the Internet. In fact, there's so much information, it can be really hard finding the stuff you need.

1) The simplest way to start researching information on the Internet is to use a search engine.
2) The basic type of search is a keyword search — you type in a keyword, and the search engine lists a load of websites containing that keyword.
3) You can do a more complex search using more than one keyword by linking them together with AND and OR. (It'll assume AND if you don't use a linking word.)
4) Alternatively, if you know the address of the web page or site you're interested in (also known as its URL — Uniform Resource Locator), you can go straight there.

The internet can be great for research

In the old days, when something went wrong in business (e.g. a cheque not arriving when it was supposed to), you were forced to make up a 'low-tech' excuse — maybe it had got lost in the post, for example. But nowadays, you can just say, 'The computer crashed.' Much more modern.

Health and Safety

Obviously you need to watch out for yourself in the workplace — and everyone else too.

Employers have to provide *safe working conditions*

1) The <u>Health and Safety at Work Act</u> (1974) was passed to make sure employers provide a <u>safe working environment</u>, and that they use <u>safety signs</u> to help reduce the risk of <u>accidents</u>.

2) Factory <u>inspectors</u> are employed to <u>examine</u> and <u>investigate</u> workplaces to check that <u>rules</u> and <u>regulations</u> are being followed.

3) There is a <u>legal obligation</u> for employers and workers to ensure that they use <u>safe working practices</u> at all times.

Risk assessments should be carried out in *workplaces*

1) An evaluation, called a <u>risk assessment</u>, must be carried out by an employer to <u>identify</u> and <u>minimise</u> any potential risks at work.

2) Risk assessments are especially important wherever <u>chemicals</u> or <u>machinery</u> are used.

3) Employers, workshop managers and your <u>technology teacher</u> must assess the risks involved at work or school, and put reasonable <u>precautions</u> in place to prevent accidents from happening. This might involve placing <u>warning</u> or <u>caution</u> <u>signs</u> on machines, installing <u>non-slip flooring</u> or putting up <u>barriers</u> and <u>guards</u>.

Remember — risk assessment identifies and minimises potential risks

Employers have a responsibility to make sure that you're safe in the workplace. But this doesn't mean that if you act unsafely and something happens to you then it's not your fault. Be responsible — if you see something that is a possible hazard then tell someone.

Health and Safety

A lot of this is common sense. But it's incredibly important, so pay attention...

Safety advice should be followed

Wear appropriate clothing

1) While working (especially with machine tools) make sure your <u>sleeves</u> are rolled back, <u>apron ties</u> are tucked in and if you've got <u>long hair</u>, it's tied back.

2) Protect yourself from <u>hazardous</u> materials by wearing strong protective <u>gloves</u> and <u>goggles</u>.

3) If <u>dust</u> or <u>vapours</u> are a danger, make sure there's adequate <u>ventilation</u>.

4) When <u>casting</u>, always wear <u>thick all-body suits</u>, <u>face visors</u>, <u>gauntlets</u> and <u>spats</u>.

Care should be taken with tools and machinery

1) Use the <u>safety guards</u> on lathes and drilling machines.

2) Know how to <u>switch off</u> and <u>isolate</u> machines in an emergency.

3) <u>Never</u> adjust a machine unless you've <u>switched it off</u> and isolated it <u>first</u>.

4) <u>Never</u> leave machines <u>unattended</u> while switched on.

5) Always <u>secure</u> work safely — e.g. you should clamp work securely for drilling.

6) Don't use <u>machines</u> or <u>hand tools</u> unless you have been <u>shown how</u>.

7) Ensure that any <u>dust extraction</u> equipment is connected and working properly.

8) <u>Carry</u> tools safely.

Handle materials and waste sensibly

1) Make sure materials are <u>safe to handle</u>. <u>Deburr</u> metal (file down any rough edges) before you start work.

2) Beware of <u>naked flames</u> or red-hot heating elements — and keep them away from <u>flammable liquids</u>.

3) Make sure you <u>dispose of waste properly</u> (this is also an environmental issue).

4) When <u>storing</u> material, make sure it's <u>put away safely</u> so it can't fall and injure anyone.

5) Never clear away metal shavings/dust with your bare hands — <u>use the brush</u> provided.

This advice is well worth learning — for your exam and your health

Companies have to take health and safety issues very seriously these days, as workers are more willing and able to sue their employers than they were in the past. Which is nice.

Warm-up and Worked Exam Questions

What is it about computers, designs and three letter acronyms? Here's five quick questions to check you've been learning along the way.

Warm-up Questions

1) How are CAD drawings shared with other computer users around the world?
2) Give a specific example of how the Internet is used in the design process.
3) Give three advantages of 3-D CAD.
4) Give an example of how 'computer rendering' can improve CAD.
5) What advantages does DTP give the graphic designer?

There's no better preparation for exam questions than doing, err, practice exam questions. Hang on, what's this I see...

Worked Exam Questions

1 a) What name is given to a 3-D full colour presentation prototype on a computer?

A virtual prototype.

(1 mark)

b) Give two different ways of inputting images into a photo-editing application.

Using a scanner.   *Other possible answers include downloading images from the Internet and importing images from other applications.*

From a digital camera.

Make sure with a question like this that you answer both parts to get the 2 marks.   *(2 marks)*

2 What does CNC stand for, and how does it work?

CNC stands for computer numerically controlled. It's when a computer describes the movements of a CAM cutter in terms of numbers.

(2 marks)

3 What is the purpose of a risk assessment?

To identify risk, and to use this knowledge of risk to minimise risk and accidents.

This question is worth 2 marks, so you need to make two points about the purpose of risk assessments.

(2 marks)

Exam Questions

4   Jude is a graphic designer who works from a small spare room at home.

   a)   Explain why a CAD system is advantageous to the storage of Jude's work.

....

(1 mark)

   b)   Name two types of media on which CAD files can be stored.

....

....

(2 marks)

5   General Print is a printing company down the road from Jude. They have large, fast-moving printing machines.

   a)   Give three examples of the sort of safety precautions individual workers can take to protect themselves when working with this type of equipment.

....

....

....

(3 marks)

   b)   Give three examples of safety precautions the employers could take to protect their workers.

....

....

....

(3 marks)

6   Give two examples of how an expensive CAM system can be cost effective.

....

....

(2 marks)

Revision Summary for Section Five

So that's it then — the end of another section. Well, you probably know what happens now... it's revision summary time. Lots of questions to check what you know, and what you don't. So keep practising them until you know all the answers. That's the best way to learn.

1) Explain the difference between good design and good manufacture.

2) Give five reasons why a consumer might choose a particular product.

3) Describe two ways a manufacturer could find out what consumers think of its product.

4) Give one reason why an evaluation is important.

5) Describe six things you could mention in your evaluation.

6) Describe five things you should think about when you're designing if you want to be socially and environmentally responsible.

7) Name three kinds of thing that can offend people if used inappropriately in a design.

8) Why are many hardwoods classed as threatened resources?

9) Explain why using a softwood is sometimes a 'greener' choice than using a hardwood.

10) Name two of the Earth's resources that are limited.

11) What happens to most waste? What problems can this cause?

12) Explain what these symbols mean: a) ♺   b) ☯

13) Explain why many companies register trademarks.

14) What is a patent? What kind of thing can be awarded a patent?

15) Explain why many companies like to get their products approved by an institute like the BSI or ISO. What does the CE mark signify?

16) Name six pieces of information that have to be on processed food labels.

17) Give seven advantages of using CAD.

18) Give three disadvantages of using CAD.

19) What is CAM? Give three advantages of using CAM, rather than the old-fashioned methods.

20) What does CNC stand for? Explain what this means.

21) Give four reasons why DTP packages have become popular.

22) Explain what is meant by a pixel.

23) Explain the difference between RGB and CMYK. When is each system used?

24) Give three advantages and three disadvantages of using ICT in industry.

25) Explain how you might go about trying to find information about a certain topic using the Internet.

26) What is the purpose of the Health and Safety at Work Act?

27) What is a risk assessment? Who should carry out risk assessments?

28) Give four precautions you should take when:
a) working with machinery,   b) handling waste.

Systems and Control

Systems comprise of <u>inputs</u>, <u>processes</u> (or <u>transformations</u>) and <u>outputs</u>. Like the digestive system, for example — that has an input (food), a process (turning food into energy) and an output (um...).

Systems transform *inputs* into *outputs*

① INPUT

<u>Inputs</u> can be anything from <u>tools</u> and <u>materials</u>, through to stuff like <u>labour</u> or <u>information</u>.

> <u>Input devices</u> include <u>keyboards</u>, <u>mice</u> and <u>scanners</u>.

② PROCESS

The <u>process</u> stage <u>transforms</u> inputs into outputs.

> <u>Processes</u> include <u>text</u> and <u>image manipulation</u> (e.g. resizing, reshaping, changing colours).

③ OUTPUT

The <u>output</u> is the <u>end product</u> of a system.

> <u>Output devices</u> include <u>monitors</u>, <u>printers</u> and <u>speakers</u>.

Examples of systems — *photocopying* and *printing*

PHOTOCOPYING

<u>Input</u>:
A4 original,
A3 paper,
toner.

<u>Process</u>:
Image
enlargement.

<u>Output</u>:
A3 copies
of the
original.

COMPUTER INK-JET / LASER PRINTING

<u>Input</u>:
Paper,
ink cartridge,
print command
from program.

<u>Process</u>:
Black or four-colour
process colour printing.

<u>Output</u>:
Hard copy
of design,
image or
artwork.

Make sure you know some examples of systems...

...and you can explain them in terms of input, process and output. Try closing the book then scribbling down the two examples shown above. If you can't remember them, then keep trying till you do.

Systems and Control

Control and feedback can be shown on a flow chart

Control describes the ability to change inputs and so alter the outputs. For example, you can change how dark an image is printed on a photocopier.

See page 67 for more about flow charts.

Feedback is a way of using the output of a system to affect the input. So if you notice that a photocopier has printed something too dark, you can change the settings and make sure the next copies are lighter.

On a flow chart, feedback is shown as a 'loop':

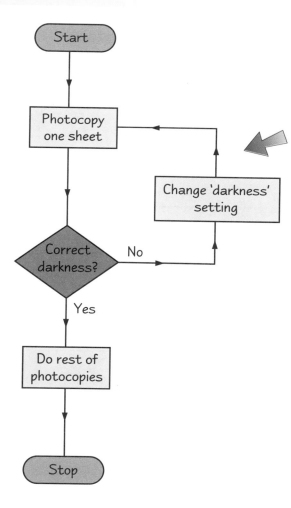

This bit is the 'feedback loop'. The decision box shows where one copy is checked, and if there's a problem, the flow chart loops back.

Control, control — you must learn control...

Loads of everyday tasks (like making a cup of tea, getting dressed, and so on) could be looked at as systems, and you could try to identify what their inputs, processes and outputs are. It'd be good practice, though I'm not really sure how interesting it would be. But that's life, I suppose.

Mechanisms

There are loads of simple <u>mechanisms</u> you can use. Some are better for <u>2-D items</u> (e.g. linkages in pop-up cards) and some for <u>3-D things</u> (e.g. cams in mechanical toys).

Mechanisms 'transfer' motion

1) <u>Mechanisms</u> involve <u>movement</u> in a <u>rotary</u> (round and round), <u>linear</u> (along a line), <u>reciprocating</u> (back and forth along a line) or <u>oscillating</u> (swinging) motion.

2) They can <u>amplify</u> or <u>reduce</u> the size of a <u>force</u> or a <u>movement</u>.

3) They can also <u>change</u> one motion (the <u>input</u>) into another (the <u>output</u>). E.g. <u>bicycle pedals</u> move in a <u>rotary</u> motion, turning the <u>wheels</u> in a <u>rotary</u> motion, moving the bicycle in a <u>linear</u> motion.

Cams rotate and move a follower

Cams are shaped pieces of material, fixed to an <u>axle</u> or <u>shaft</u>. As they <u>rotate</u>, they make a '<u>follower</u>' move in a <u>linear</u> / <u>reciprocating</u> fashion.

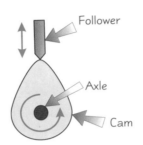

There are three classes of lever

Each class has a <u>load</u>, <u>effort</u> and <u>fulcrum</u> (or pivot point).

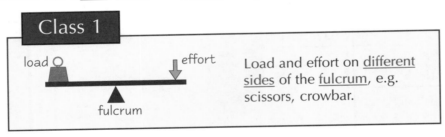

Class 1

Load and effort on <u>different sides</u> of the <u>fulcrum</u>, e.g. scissors, crowbar.

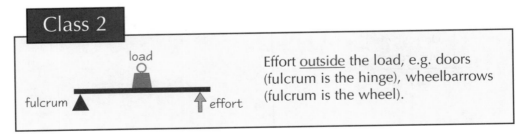

Class 2

Effort <u>outside</u> the load, e.g. doors (fulcrum is the hinge), wheelbarrows (fulcrum is the wheel).

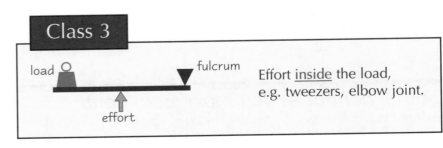

Class 3

Effort <u>inside</u> the load, e.g. tweezers, elbow joint.

Mechanisms

Linkages can transfer forces

Linkages are great for...

① ...transferring a force, e.g. lazy tongs...

lazy tongs are used for moving things whilst keeping them at a distance and for picking things up

② ...turning a push force into a pull...

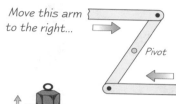

Move this arm to the right...

Pivot

...and this arm moves to the left.

③ ...and allowing objects to have a telescopic mechanism.

Pulleys have wheels and a belt

Pulleys are grooved wheels with a belt or rope round them.

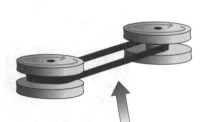

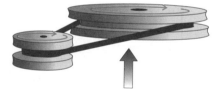

① They can <u>transfer energy</u>...

② ...<u>reverse the direction</u> of rotation (by putting a twist in the belt)...

③ ...or can <u>make lifting heavy loads easier</u> (by using wheels of different sizes).

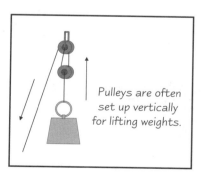

Pulleys are often set up vertically for lifting weights.

Cams, levers, linkages and pulleys make life easier

You can make these mechanisms out of card. Make holes in the card using a bradawl (with a piece of wood underneath). And use paper fasteners or eyelets to make pivots or to join card linkages together.

Scale of Production

The term 'scale of production' is all about the <u>quantity</u> of products that you're going to manufacture. Commercially there are <u>four main categories</u> for you to learn...

Jobbing production — making a **one-off** product

1) This is where you're making a <u>single product</u>.

2) Every item made will be different, to meet the customer's <u>individual</u> and <u>specific requirements</u>.

3) This type of production is very <u>labour-intensive</u>, and requires a <u>highly skilled</u> workforce.

4) Examples are wide-ranging, from made-to-measure furniture to bridges, power stations, jewellery and sculptures.

Batch production — a **specified quantity** of a product

1) This is where you're making a <u>specific quantity</u> of a particular product.

2) Batches can be <u>repeated</u> as many times as required.

3) The <u>machinery</u> and <u>labour</u> used need to be <u>flexible</u>, so they can quickly change from making one batch to making another batch of a similar product.

4) The time <u>between</u> batches, when machines and tools may have to be set up differently or changed around, is called <u>down time</u>. This is <u>unproductive</u> and needs to be kept as short as possible so the manufacturer doesn't lose money.

Bread, books and CDs are all made in batches.

Continuous production — **non-stop** production 24 hrs a day

1) This involves <u>non-stop</u>, uninterrupted production.

2) The specialised equipment required costs so much that it would be too <u>expensive</u> to turn it off. So it has to keep running and producing continuously.

3) Examples of continuous production include <u>oil</u> and <u>chemical</u> manufacture.

4) This type of production needs workers that have been specially <u>trained</u> to used the equipment.

Scale of Production

Mass production — high-volume production

1) Making products on a really <u>large scale</u>, such as cars or electrical goods.

2) Often uses <u>expensive specialised equipment</u> including computer-aided manufacturing (CAM) and industrial robots.

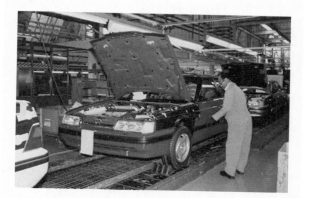

3) As well as all this equipment, you need a <u>large workforce</u>. The different stages of production and manufacture are <u>broken down</u> into simple <u>repetitive tasks</u> which people are able to learn easily.

4) <u>Recruitment</u> is relatively <u>easy</u> — you don't need to employ skilled people.

5) <u>In-line assembly</u> is often used for mass production.

Cell production — small teams produce one whole unit

1) The <u>workforce</u> is arranged into '<u>cells</u>' or teams. Each cell is responsible for making a whole unit.

2) The idea is that working in cells encourages better <u>teamwork</u>. Each worker in the cell is usually trained to carry out all the tasks the cell does.

3) It's often used as a way of organising work in <u>mass production</u> factories.

> <u>Logistics</u> is about the <u>organisation</u> of materials, machinery, staff and other <u>resources</u> needed to get the product made.
> How a manufacturer decides to produce their goods affects their logistics set-up.

Just-in-time manufacturing needs detailed forward planning

For <u>just-in-time</u> manufacturing (JIT), you only buy materials and components as and <u>when you need them</u>. The components are delivered, made into products straight away, then are delivered to customers.

ADVANTAGES:

1) There is no need to store <u>large stockpiles of resources</u> in warehouses. This <u>saves money</u> and space.

2) Better <u>cash flow</u> — capital is not tied up in stock.

3) <u>Less waste</u> — no old or damaged stock lying around.

4) <u>Greater flexibility</u>, as products are built to order.

DISADVANTAGES:

1) <u>Supplier delays</u> can <u>halt production</u> — no stored stock to use.

2) <u>Strikes</u> halt supply to customers — no finished stock to send out.

3) Can't respond to a <u>sudden increase</u> in demand — no raw material stocks.

4) Products need to be <u>right first time</u> — no extra stock to replace faulty products.

Just-in-time — needs a fine balance

This page isn't too bad — make sure you've memorised the details of mass production and you understand the advantages and disadvantages of JIT manufacturing.

Commercial Products and Packaging

It's useful to look at commercial packaging and try to work out how <u>manufacturers</u> could have made it. It could give you <u>ideas</u> for stuff that you have to make <u>yourself</u>.

Packaging for a **mobile phone**

Packaging for a <u>mobile phone</u> may comprise:

① A <u>die-cut carton board</u> box (see page 102).

② A vacuum-formed rigid <u>polystyrene</u> tray.

③ A <u>paper</u> sleeve printed in full colour using the four process colours by <u>offset lithography</u>, and with <u>embossed</u> and <u>varnished</u> special effects to enhance the logo and photograph of the product.

A **T-shirt** with packaging

1) A design can be <u>applied</u> to the T-shirt using the <u>screen printing</u> process or <u>iron-on vinyl</u> cut by a Roland Camm machine.
2) It can be <u>packaged</u> in an <u>extruded polyethylene</u> bag printed using <u>flexography</u>, and with a <u>die-cut cardboard</u> header to aid hanging.

Packaging for **milk**

Milk can be packaged in a number of convenient forms:

1) In blow-moulded <u>HDPE</u> (see page 22) containers with an injection-moulded HDPE screw cap and tamper-evident seal.
2) In <u>die-cut waxed card</u> Tetra Pak cartons.
3) In blow-moulded, reusable <u>glass</u> bottles with a <u>die-cut aluminium foil</u> seal.

Registration marks are used by *printers*

These can take a number of forms and be used for different purposes:

<u>Colour registration marks</u> are used by printers to check the <u>colour density</u> and the position or <u>alignment</u> of one colour relative to another. They are usually square blocks or concentric circles.

<u>Crop marks</u> are used by printers to show where a printed page needs to be <u>cut to size</u> (guillotined).

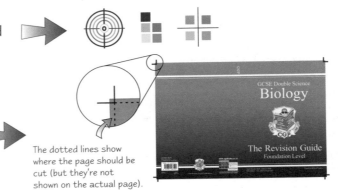

The dotted lines show where the page should be cut (but they're not shown on the actual page).

The type of packaging depends on the product

If you're feeling bored one day, take a number of everyday products and try to work out what they're made of and what production and printing processes were used. Do they have any registration marks?

Packaging and Waste

Packaging <u>protects</u>, <u>preserves</u> and <u>promotes</u> the product it contains.

Protection — during **transit** and from **customers**

1) Packaging materials like cardboard and expanded polystyrene can <u>protect</u> a product from knocks and bumps during <u>transportation</u>.
2) Manufacturers can also add <u>tamper-evident seals</u> to packaging to try and prevent customers tampering with products.

Preservation — especially **foodstuffs**

1) Many products (especially <u>foodstuffs</u>) begin to <u>deteriorate</u> when exposed to <u>oxygen</u> in the air.
2) Sealed <u>glass jars</u> and <u>bottles</u>, <u>'tin' cans</u> and <u>tubes</u> are traditional packages for foodstuffs, drinks and toothpaste.
3) However, <u>plastics</u> and <u>composite materials</u> (e.g. layers of card, plastic and aluminium foil laminated together) are being used more and more these days.

Promotion — to make you **buy more stuff**

1) Manufacturers often use striking <u>colours</u> and <u>shapes</u> of packaging to <u>entice</u> you to <u>buy</u> their products.
2) As well as the names of the <u>manufacturer</u> and the <u>product</u>, the packaging may include pictures or images showing <u>how</u> the product should be <u>used</u>, or a <u>contact address</u> (or anything else for that matter).
3) It may also include a <u>'flash'</u> showing <u>money off</u> or a catchy <u>slogan</u>, e.g. '*CGP — Buy our books, they're ace*'.

Avoid unnecessary waste with the **3 Rs**

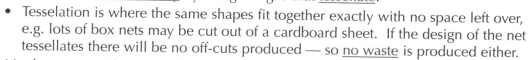

<u>Unnecessary</u> and <u>waste</u> packaging is a big problem.
But there are things the <u>public</u> and <u>industry</u> can do to help.

REDUCTION — Use materials <u>economically</u> by using designs that <u>tessellate</u>.
- Tesselation is where the same shapes fit together exactly with no space left over, e.g. lots of box nets may be cut out of a cardboard sheet. If the design of the net tessellates there will be no off-cuts produced — so <u>no waste</u> is produced either.
— It's also a smart idea to <u>avoid</u> unnecessary packaging, e.g. by selling chocolates in a <u>paper bag</u> rather than a plastic tray in a cardboard box wrapped in cellophane.

REUSING — Milk bottles, jam jars and egg boxes can be <u>reused</u> many times.

RECYCLING — Recycling materials (e.g. card, glass, plastic, metal) means they can be used again to make the <u>same</u> or <u>different</u> products.

Remember the 3 Rs — Reduction, Reusing, Recycling
Packaging is used to protect, preserve and promote the product, but the more packaging, the more waste is produced... and that's bad for the environment. Manufacturers can do their bit by reducing the packaging and making it recyclable. You can do your bit by reusing packaging like jam jars.

Printing Methods

Designers and manufacturers use various <u>commercial printing methods</u>.
And because I know you're desperate to know about them, I've included two whole pages on them.

Letterpress uses a *flat* printing plate

1) This is a form of <u>relief printing</u> — meaning the <u>image</u> or <u>type</u> (i.e. the text) is <u>raised above</u> the flat printing plate.

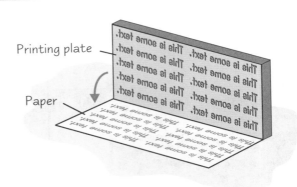

Printing plate

Paper

2) It's used for the printing of large amounts of <u>monochrome</u> (i.e. one-colour) text — e.g. books, headed paper and business cards.

3) Letterpress is ideal for <u>print runs</u> of 500-5000 copies, but can do fewer.

Flexography uses a *cylindrical* printing plate

1) <u>Flexography</u> is a similar method to letterpress.

2) However, the printing plate is made from plastic or rubber <u>cylinders</u>.

3) It's a <u>quick</u> process and is used for large print runs, making it ideal for printing packaging, carrier bags and wallpaper.

Gravure uses an *etched* printing plate

1) Gravure uses an <u>etched</u> printing plate, meaning the image is <u>lower</u> than the surface of the plate.

2) This process is used to produce <u>quality products</u> such as magazines, books and postage stamps.

3) It's an <u>expensive</u> process, but is ideal for very large print runs — half a million copies or more.

High quality magazines and stamps

Letterpress = flat, flexography = cylindrical, gravure = etched... easy
Once you get your head round what type of plate each method uses, it's really easy to figure out what they are used to produce.

Printing Methods

Lithography and offset lithography use 'oily' ink

1) Lithography works on the principle of <u>oil</u> and <u>water</u> not mixing.

2) An aluminium <u>printing plate</u> has a <u>relief</u> (i.e. raised) image transferred to it photographically using ultraviolet light.

3) The plate is washed with a chemical that makes the <u>image</u> area <u>attract</u> ink, while the <u>non-image</u> area is kept <u>wet</u> (and so <u>repels</u> the 'oily' ink).

4) Lithography's an <u>economical</u> printing process, ideal for print runs of 1000 copies and upwards — so is used to print books, posters, magazines, packaging...

5) In <u>offset lithography</u>, the image is first printed onto a rubber <u>'blanket'</u> cylinder, and this blanket cylinder transfers the image to the paper.

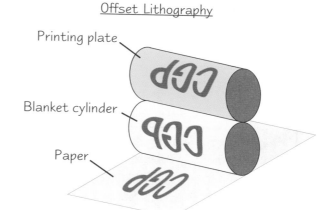

Offset Lithography

Printing plate

Blanket cylinder

Paper

Screen printing uses a screen

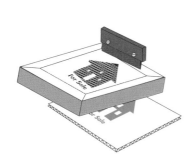

1) This is a <u>low-cost</u> process.

2) It is ideal for <u>short</u> print runs (of up to a few hundred copies) where <u>fine detail</u> is not required.

3) It's possible to print onto various <u>surfaces</u> — e.g. paper, card, fabric and corriflute (the plastic stuff they make estate agents' signs from), so is ideal for printing posters, T-shirts, wallpaper, estate agents' signs...

Learn how each type of printing works

And learn what each one is good for, e.g. what type would you use to print stamps?.. or T-shirts? There are only five types so you've got no excuse not to learn it all. Don't forget that these printing methods are used in industry — you'll probably only use inkjet or laser printers at home or school.

Surface Effects

Special effects can be used to make graphic products look fancier.

Die cutting is used for cutting and creasing

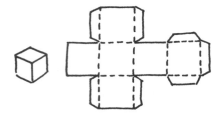

1) Die cutting uses a series of knives and folding/creasing bars fixed to a plywood base.

2) These are aligned so that they cut out and crease nets (shape nets, that is — not the stringy kind) for packaging, point-of-sale displays, etc.

3) As many nets as possible are cut out of the same sheet of card at the same time to reduce costs.

Embossing leaves a raised impression

1) Embossing means pushing a shaped die into a piece of paper or card from behind, leaving a raised impression on its surface.

2) It's used to draw attention to a particular bit of the product, e.g. book title, logo or image.

3) It's an expensive process but adds texture and can suggest quality.

Foil application makes things look fancy

1) Foil application (or foil blocking) means 'printing' metal foil onto certain areas of a product.

2) It's often used in packaging to draw attention to a logo, brand name, etc.

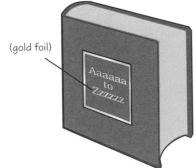

(gold foil)

3) Again, it's an expensive process but can give the impression of quality.

Try using embossing and foil application to make your work fancy

These are all ways to make things look fancy. And this is vital, because image is everything these days. You might even be able to use some of these effects in your project, and make your idea stand out from the work that your friends have produced. But don't tell them I said that.

Surface Effects

Laminating means sandwiching in plastic

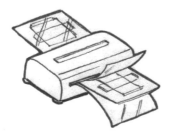

1) <u>Laminating</u> is the process of <u>sandwiching</u> thin layers of material together. Often it's used to sandwich a document (e.g. a poster, menu or business card) between two layers of <u>plastic</u>.

2) This is done by passing the document and the plastic covers through the <u>heated rollers</u> of a laminating machine.

3) Many <u>packaging materials</u> are a lamination of different papers, cards, plastics and aluminium foil.

4) The aim is usually to make the surface better for <u>printing</u> on, or to form a <u>barrier</u> against oxygen or moisture.

Varnishing makes things look shiny

1) <u>Varnishing</u> is a <u>printing effect</u> that's added after all the other colours are printed and dry.

2) <u>Four types</u> of varnish are used — oil-based, water-based, spirit-based and ultraviolet.

3) Varnishing can be applied over the <u>whole product</u> or just <u>specific areas</u> (called spot varnishing) that need <u>highlighting</u> — e.g. photographs and headings on packaging, catalogues or books.

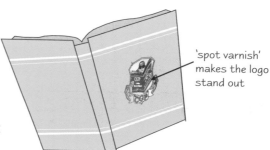

'spot varnish' makes the logo stand out

Modern photocopiers can do all kinds of fancy stuff

1) Modern photocopiers can <u>duplicate</u>, <u>enlarge</u> and <u>reduce</u> documents onto thin <u>card</u> and <u>acetate</u>, as well as a variety of <u>papers</u>.

2) Photocopying can help in the <u>development</u> of a design where an <u>outline</u> of an object needs to be quickly and easily reproduced.

3) Photocopiers can also <u>collate</u> and <u>staple</u> multi-page documents together.

Photocopiers — duplicate, enlarge and reduce documents

Remember, you've got to do good work in the first place — you can't just come up with any old bit of work and try and make it good by adding fancy bits. If your work is good in the first place then adding fancy effects will make it extra good.

Production Methods

There are different things you can do to make production easier, faster and more efficient...

CAD/CAM — Computer-Aided Design / Manufacture

Computer-Aided Design (CAD, see p.81) and Computer-Aided Manufacture (CAM, see p.82) are being used more and more in the production of graphic products — both in industry and schools.

CAD packages work by converting lines, shapes and text to sets of coordinates. These coordinates are then interpreted by the CAM machine as lines to cut out, plot or print.

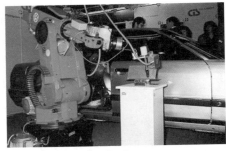

CAM machines can cut, score and print designs onto card, vinyl and other materials, making it easy to produce labels, printed T-shirts, stencils and signs.

A robotic arm controlled by CAM

Jigs, templates and moulds improve accuracy

Various devices can be used while making goods to save time and improve accuracy. Examples include jigs, templates and moulds. They're very important in industry.

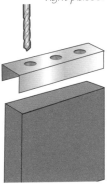

This kind of jig fits over the end of the plank and makes it easy to drill the holes in the right places.

1) Jigs are used to position or align materials for drilling and sawing wood, scoring and folding card and so on.

2) Templates are things you can draw or cut around to achieve consistency of shape and size.

3) Moulds, patterns and formers are used to make single items, or numerous copies of something, e.g. when vacuum forming.

Jigs, templates, moulds and CAD/CAM make production faster

If you need to draw lots of identical shapes for your project then it's a good idea to make a template first, even if it does take you a few minutes.

Scanners and Barcodes

Scanners can transfer images onto a computer

1) <u>Scanners</u> are used to <u>convert</u> photographs, pictures and hand-drawn images into <u>computer files</u> that can be <u>manipulated</u> using <u>graphics packages</u>.

2) These allow the user to <u>resize</u> images, change <u>colours</u> and add various <u>effects</u>.

3) The images produced can then be used in <u>desktop publishing</u> packages or <u>word processors</u>.

Barcodes are pretty much everywhere nowadays

1) <u>Barcodes</u> are sets of vertical black and white <u>lines</u> (bars) of <u>varying thickness</u> that can be read by a <u>scanner</u> (or reader).

2) The thickness of the bars and the spaces between them correspond to <u>numbers</u> that make up a unique <u>code</u> for each type of product.

3) You see them on all kinds of goods these days, including CDs, books and food.

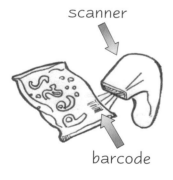

scanner

barcode

4) Hand-held and till-mounted <u>optical scanners</u> are used in some shops to read <u>barcodes</u> as goods are sold.

5) It means that shop staff don't have to <u>remember</u> individual prices. They also make it easier to <u>record</u> sales, and to <u>control</u> stock levels and reordering.

6) The information obtained can also be used for <u>marketing</u> purposes.

Barcodes — but why... they're really handy...

Barcodes make it really easy for shops to track stock levels. This means they know exactly how many they have sold and how many they have left on the shelves or in the warehouse.

Warm-up and Worked Exam Questions

By the time the big day comes you need to know all the facts in these warm-up questions and all the exam questions. Hang on in there, the end is in sight.

Warm-up Questions

1) What names do we give to the three main sections of a control system?
2) What are the 3 Ps of packaging?
3) What shape printing plate does flexography printing use?
4) What's used on the non-printing part of a lithography printing plate to stop ink sticking to it?
5) What's a jig used for?

This is the last set of exam questions before the practice exam.
So make an extra big effort and do us proud.

Worked Exam Question

1   Ballmark are designers and manufacturers of greetings cards. They can print 20 greetings cards on an A0 size sheet of card. The design of the greetings cards includes a circular shape window on the front, which needs to be cut out.

a) What name is given to the machine tool used to cut out nets / surface developments when they are made on a commercial scale?

Die cutting machine.

(1 mark)

b) When manufacturing products in quantity, there are four different scales of production. What are they?

One-off production (jobbing), batch production,

mass production and continuous production.

(4 marks)

c) Some of Ballmark's production equipment uses pulleys to make different parts of the machine move together.

What is needed to transfer energy from pulley to pulley in a mechanical system?

Belts.

Pulleys can also be used to reverse direction and to make lifting heavy loads easier.

(1 mark)

Exam Questions

2   XYZ are a printing company. Their next printing job is the packaging for 'Perfect Blend' tea bags. XYZ have the job of printing and preparing the packages, ready for assembly. 16 separate packages will be printed onto a sheet of A0 card. Each of the 16 nets (surface development) for the Perfect Blend packaging, will then be cut out with a die.

    a)   Why would XYZ try to get as many nets as possible out of one sheet of card?

....

(1 mark)

    b)   If a combination of embossing and foil blocking was added to the package design, what impression would this create on the potential customers of Perfect Blend tea?

....

....

(2 marks)

3   XYZ are also manufacturing a Christmas card, like the one below, where the Santa is able to move up and down the chimney.

    a)   What type of mechanism could be used to produce the movement shown?

....

(1 mark)

    b)   On the diagram above, sketch the mechanism needed to move the Santa up and down the chimney.

(3 marks)

    c)   On your sketched diagram, label the following items:

       i)   fixed pivot.

       ii)   moving pivots.

(2 marks)

Revision Summary for Section Six

That's the end of another section... and you know what that means... yep, revision questions. This was a pretty easy section so you shouldn't have any problems in answering the questions below. If you do then have a quick look back through the section and try again. Keep going... only one more section to go after this.

1) What are the three things that make up a system?

2) Name two computer input devices and two computer output devices.

3) What is 'control' in a system?

4) Describe how feedback works. How is feedback shown on a flow chart?

5) Name four kinds of mechanism.

6) Describe the three classes of lever.

7) Describe three uses of: a) linkages, and b) pulleys.

8) List the four main scales of production.

9) Explain what 'just-in-time production' is.

10) What are crop marks used for? And registration marks?

11) Explain the difference between letterpress printing and flexography.

12) Explain briefly how lithography and offset lithography work.

13) Name three surfaces you can use screen printing on.

14) Describe the following:
a) die cutting, b) embossing, c) laminating, d) varnishing.

15) Apart from copying an image, name three other functions a photocopier can perform.

16) Explain what is meant by CAD/CAM.

17) How can jigs improve accuracy in manufacturing?

18) Name two advantages of using barcodes.

19) Describe the three purposes of packaging.

20) Explain three ways in which waste can be limited.

Tips on Getting Started

This section's got all the things that exam boards criticise people for <u>not doing</u>.
Read this before you start your project to make sure you don't throw away marks.

Step 1 — *Get your idea*

You can get ideas from <u>different</u> places — for example, your teacher might:

- <u>Tell</u> you exactly what your task is.

- Give you a <u>range</u> of tasks to choose from.

- Leave the project <u>choice</u> completely up to you.

Don't choose anything *too easy* or *too boring*

Choose a project that will:

1) <u>Stretch</u> you and let you <u>demonstrate</u> just how <u>good</u> you are. If the project's too <u>easy</u>, or contains little scope for design, then you'll <u>lose</u> valuable marks.

2) Be <u>interesting</u> and <u>challenging</u> enough to keep you <u>motivated</u>. Coursework's a <u>long</u> old process, and you need to stay <u>committed</u>.

3) Give you the opportunity to produce a <u>wide range</u> of <u>research</u>, and demonstrate your <u>ICT</u> skills.

4) Allow for a <u>variety</u> of solutions, resulting in a project which can be completed <u>before the deadline</u> (and this includes allowing time for <u>testing</u> and <u>evaluation</u>).

The *design brief* — give *loads* of *detail*

See page 5 for more on the design brief.

1) Your idea needs to have <u>real commercial potential</u>.

2) You need to describe <u>exactly</u> what you're trying to do.

3) <u>Explain all the factors</u> you need to consider — things like price, weight, market trends, etc.

Think hard before you start — you'll regret choosing a dull project...

It might seem like a ridiculous idea, but try and choose a project that doesn't bore you to tears. You're much more likely to produce higher quality work, and get higher marks.

Tips on Getting Started

You need to be <u>organised</u> and <u>methodical</u> when you're compiling your research. It'll save you a lot of time when you come to writing up your research analysis.

Say *why* your *research* is *relevant*

1) <u>DON'T</u> put bits of paper in your research folder without any explanation.

2) <u>DON'T</u> just copy and paste stuff from the Internet.

3) <u>DO</u> <u>write notes</u> on <u>every</u> piece of research to say <u>why</u> it's <u>relevant</u>, how it changed your thinking or how it backed up your existing ideas.

4) <u>DO</u> <u>refer back</u> to the research section <u>throughout the project</u> — that helps to show you've <u>used your research</u>.

This is all you need to do:

See page 6 for more on research.

Print or photocopy the relevant stuff.

This is my clever and interesting research that I got off the Internet. This is my clever and interesting research that I got off the Internet. This is my clever and interesting research that I got off the Internet. This is my clever and interesting research that I got off the Internet. This is my clever and interesting that I got off the Internet. This is my clever and interesting research that I got off the Internet. This is my clever and interesting research that I got off the Internet.

Highlight the really useful bits.

Write brief notes saying where you found it...

...what you found out...

I found this on the Clever and Interesting Website (www.clever.co.uk).
The highlighted part explains how the cleverness affects the interestingness of products. I hadn't previously considered these effects so I will now incorporate the use of different materials into my testing.

...and what effect it's had on your project.

<u>Remember</u> — your <u>research analysis</u> will contain all the <u>conclusions</u> from research. But these notes will help you write that research analysis, and will also help the examiner understand why you made your decisions.

Three BIG reasons why research is important...

1) It helps you to get started and solidify your ideas. 2) Presenting your research well shows the examiners you know what you're doing. 3) It helps to direct your project as you go along.

Tips on Development

If you're smart you'll keep planning and evaluating throughout your project.
If you're daft you'll do a bit at the start, then forget about it and get a bad mark for your project.

You need a **wide range** of ideas — be **creative**

1) There's <u>more</u> than <u>one way</u> of doing your project well.

2) Consider <u>plenty</u> of <u>different ways</u> to <u>solve</u> the problem.

3) <u>Don't</u> just come up with <u>one good idea</u> and stick with it.
   You'll only be sure it's the <u>best</u> idea if you've <u>thought about other ways</u> of doing it.

4) The examiners do really get <u>annoyed</u> about this one — so get those creative juices flowing.

Developing your **ideas** — try out a few **alternatives**

1) The same goes for <u>developing</u> ideas as for <u>creating</u> them — there's lots of different things you could do.

2) Once you've got the idea, there are still <u>plenty</u> of ways to turn it into a <u>good product</u>.

Do **loads** of **planning** — and **not just** at the **start**

Planning is for life, not just for the start of your project.
These are the things you should do:

OVERALL PROJECT PLAN AT THE START:

Having an overall plan will help you <u>focus</u> on the task. You need to make sure you know what stage you should have reached at any time — this way, if you fall behind schedule, you'll know about it as soon as possible, and can <u>do something about it</u>. You also need to allow enough time for <u>all</u> the different stages of the design process — including testing, evaluation, and writing up your project.

PLAN YOUR RESEARCH:

Work out what <u>research</u> you need to do, and how long you're going to allow yourself for each bit (e.g. questionnaires, disassembling a competing product, and so on).

DON'T GET BOGGED DOWN:

When you're generating proposals or developing your product, don't spend too long working on one little aspect of the product. There's a lot to do — so try to keep your project moving forward.

Be realistic about how long things will take you to do

Remember to leave time for testing and evaluating in your time plan. It's all too easy to forget them.

Tips on Evaluation

<u>Evaluation</u> means <u>examining</u> and <u>judging</u> your work (and <u>you</u> have to do this as part of your project — it's not just something for the examiner to do). If your product doesn't work, but you explain <u>why</u>, you can still get <u>good marks</u>.

Test and **evaluate** your product **throughout** the **project**

Quote from one of the Chief Examiners' Reports.

> *"To be achieving the highest marks in this section, candidates must show that they have used a clear and objective testing strategy."*

i.e. it's important.

Don't wait until you're **finished** to **evaluate** your work

1) Like any designer, it's a good idea to be thinking about <u>evaluation</u> from the moment you <u>start</u> working on your <u>design brief</u>.

2) Make <u>notes</u> on your <u>designs</u> and <u>developments</u> as you go along, explaining what was <u>good</u> and <u>bad</u> about each one.

3) When you're writing up your <u>final evaluation</u>, you can also think about whether you'd do anything <u>differently</u> if you were starting again. It's okay if you made some <u>bad decisions</u> during your project — everyone does. But you can get marks if you <u>explain why</u> they were bad decisions, and what you <u>wish</u> you'd done instead.

Check your **brief** and **specification**

You need to evaluate your product <u>fully</u>. Use these guidelines:

1) <u>Compare</u> your final product to your <u>brief</u> and <u>specification</u>. Does your product satisfy all the conditions it's supposed to? If not, why not?

2) Try to get a <u>likely user</u> (or an expert in this kind of product, maybe) to <u>trial</u> your product and give their <u>honest opinions</u>. This will give you a <u>realistic view</u> of whether it's <u>fit for its purpose</u> — e.g. does it do what it's meant to? And if it does, how well? They may also be able to give you ideas for improvements.

3) It's also dead important to think about things you could have done better, such as...

    1) <u>Time implications</u> — did you spend too much time in one area, or rush to finish?

    2) <u>Practical work</u> — were you completely <u>satisfied</u> with the <u>quality</u> of your final product?

    3) Would you <u>approach</u> aspects of your design and development work in a <u>different</u> way?

You can make mistakes and get marks — all at the same time...
Everyone makes mistakes. So don't worry too much when it happens to you.
Just explain what went wrong and how you'd avoid it in the future. You can get marks for that.

Tips on Presentation

It's no use doing a brilliant project if your presentation's poor. You've put a lot of time and effort into your project (probably) so it would be a shame for you to mess it up at the last stage. It really is worth putting in those few extra hours.

The finished product — good photographs are important

Your evaluation should be clearly presented and easy to read.

1) Include an introduction to give a bit of background information — e.g. how you came to think of the project.

2) Always take photos of any non-permanent work or intermediate stages in making the product. You can use either a normal or a digital camera and then either glue in the print or place the digital image into a word-processed document — whatever suits.

> Photos are the only way of getting a lasting record of your work — and the examiners REALLY WANT you to do it.

3) Use a mixture of media to present your project. It's always good to show off how nifty you are with CAD or that desktop publishing program, but don't forget about old-fashioned words to explain what you did, and sketches and prototypes to show how you did it.

4) Split up your evaluation into different sections to make it easy to read. Give each section a clear heading.

The sections could include:

a) how well your product satisfies the brief and specification

b) results from user trials

c) problems you encountered

d) improvements for the future

5) Think about how it fits together — your project needs to work as a whole. It should flow seamlessly from one bit to the next — don't just shove loads of separate bits in with no clue as to how they fit together.

Vocabulary — use the right technical terms

BIG, FANCY WORDS:

1) Do yourself a favour — learn all the technical terms.
2) And how to spell them.
3) And don't worry if you sound fancy.
4) Using the right technical terms impresses the examiners. They say so in their reports.

GRAMMAR, SPELLING, PUNCTUATION:

1) Treat your project like an English essay.
2) Get your spellings right. Double-check any words you often get wrong.
3) Remember to use full stops and capital letters and write in proper sentences.
4) Short sentences make your work clearer. Long sentences, with loads of commas, can often get very confusing, because it's easy, once you get to the end of the sentence, to forget what you were reading right at the start.
5) Structure your work in paragraphs — a new paragraph for a new topic.

You've done all the work — take time to show you've done it...

This is the time to really clock up those marks. And be experimental and creative when you're doing it. The aim is to make your project and your work easy to understand and attractive.

Summary Checklist

This stuff can really make your project a <u>winner</u>.
That's why I've given it a whole extra page — so you can't forget <u>any</u> of it.
Before you hand in your project, make sure you've covered all of these bits,
and you'll be well on your way to D&T heaven.

Project Checklist

☐ 1) My design brief details what the problem is.

☐ 2) I've done plenty of research, and said why it's relevant.

☐ 3) I've made a detailed design specification.

☐ 4) I've come up with a wide range of project proposals.

☐ 5) I've included different ways of developing my product, and explained why I made my decisions.

6) I've done loads of planning, including:

☐ a) a production plan (time plan),

☐ b) planning for mass production.

☐ 7) I've tested my product on consumers.

☐ 8) I've evaluated my product throughout the project.

☐ 9) I've taken photos of intermediate stages and anything that won't last.

☐ 10) I've used a mixture of media to present my project.

☐ 11) I've checked my spelling and grammar.

☐ 12) I've used the right technical terms.

Practice Exam

Once you've been through all the questions in this book, you should feel pretty confident about the exam. As final preparation, here is a **practice exam** to really get you set for the real thing. This paper is designed to give you the best possible preparation for the differing question styles of the actual exams, whichever syllabus you're following. If you're doing Foundation then you won't have learnt every bit — but it's still good practice.

General Certificate of Secondary Education

GCSE
Design and Technology
Graphic Products

Centre name					
Centre number					
Candidate number					

Time allowed: 2 hours

Surname	
Other names	
Candidate signature	

In addition to this paper you will need:
- Drawing equipment
- Coloured pencils
- 45/60 degree set squares may also be used

Instructions to candidates
- Write your name and other details in the spaces provided above.
- Answer **all** questions in the spaces provided.
- Use blue or black ink or ball-point pen.

Information for candidates
- The marks available are given in brackets at the end of each question or part-question.
- The total number of marks available for this paper is **109**.
- There are **8** questions in this paper. There are no blank pages.
- Measurements are in millimetres unless stated otherwise.

Advice to candidates
- Work steadily through the paper.
- Include diagrams where they may be helpful.
- In calculations show clearly how you work out your answers.

116

1   A drawing of a logo design is shown opposite.

To print this logo, three printing plates are
required. (one for BLACK, one for MAGENTA,
one for CYAN)
The BLACK printing plate is shown completed
below.

LOGO

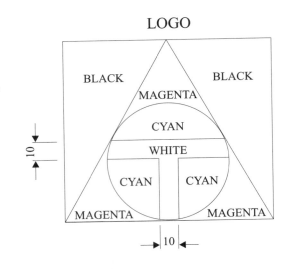

(a) (i) Complete the MAGENTA plate.

Show clearly the areas to be printed
magenta and those to be masked off.

(3 marks)

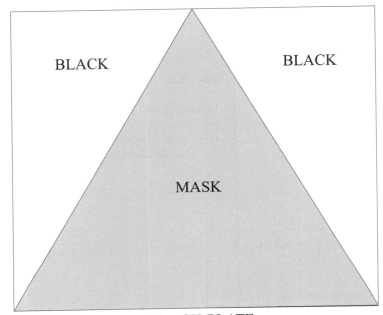

BLACK PLATE

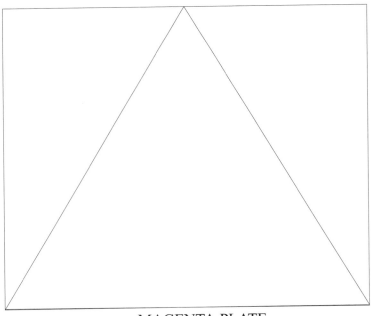

MAGENTA PLATE

(ii) Complete the CYAN plate.

Show clearly the areas to be printed cyan and those to be masked off.

(3 marks)

CYAN PLATE

(b) Give the more common names for CYAN and MAGENTA.

CYAN ....
(1 mark)

MAGENTA ....
(1 mark)

(c) The logo has been designed in the USA.
The printing will be done in the UK.
State how ICT has helped:

(i) the designers to communicate the designs to the printing company;

....
(1 mark)

(ii) with the printing of the logo.

....
(1 mark)

OCR, JUNE 2003

2   A Product Analysis chart for three items included in a children's activity pack is shown below.
The Product Analysis of the DOT to DOT and the JIGSAW has been completed.
In the spaces provided, complete the Product Analysis for the SELF ASSEMBLY CARD MODEL.

PRODUCT	TARGET AGE GROUP	MATERIALS
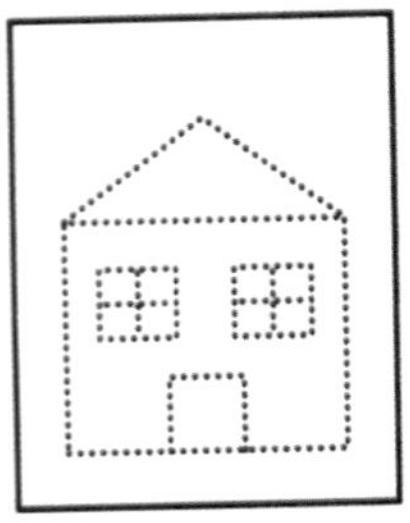 DOT TO DOT	SUITABLE FOR CHILDREN UPTO THE AGE OF 11. OLDER CHILDREN WOULD THEN BECOME BORED WITH THIS TYPE OF PRODUCT.	A4 PAPER WITH ONE OR MORE DESIGNS PRINTED ONTO THE SHEET. POSSIBILITY OF USING RECYCLED PAPER.
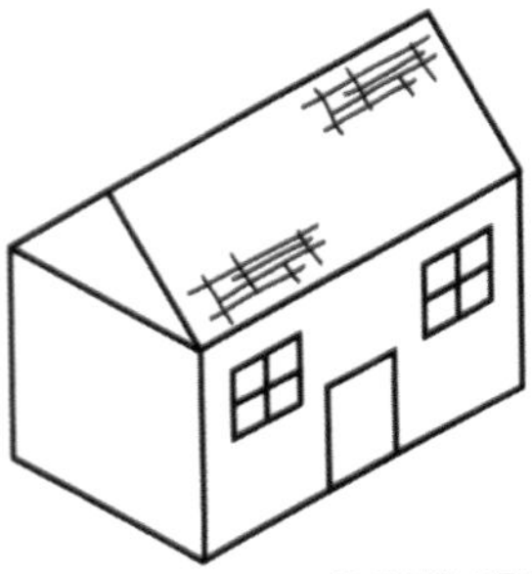 SELF ASSEMBLY CARD MODEL	*(2 marks)*	*(2 marks)*
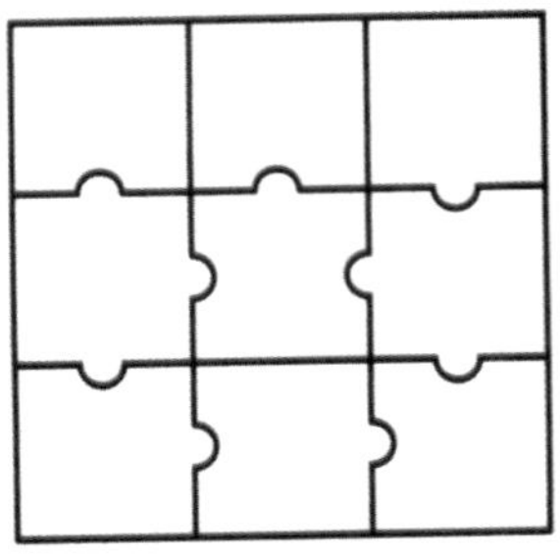 JIGSAW	SUITABLE FOR YOUNG CHILDREN IF LARGE PIECES USED. OLDER CHILDREN NEED SMALLER PIECES AND MORE COMPLEX DESIGNS.	LAMINATED BOARD PRINTED ONTO TOP SURFACE ONLY. HIGH QUALITY TOP LAYER WITH RECYCLED LAYERS IN MIDDLE.

MANUFACTURE	QUALITY CONTROL	HEALTH AND SAFETY
THE DESIGNS ARE HAND DRAWN AND SCANNED INTO A GRAPHICS PACKAGE SUCH AS PHOTOSHOP OR COREL DRAW. THIS WILL MAKE IT EASIER TO PRODUCE PLATES.	DOTS SHOULD MATCH THE DESIGN. PRINT QUALITY.	NO APPARENT RISKS.
(2 marks)	*(2 marks)*	*(2 marks)*
FULL COLOUR OFFSET LITHO PRINTING WITH PROGRAMMABLE DIE CUTTING OF PIECES TO ALLOW FOR HIGH VOLUME PRODUCTION.	PIECES LINE UP WHEN CUT OUT TO ENSURE PICTURE LOOKS RIGHT.	WARNING ON BOX TO MAKE PARENTS AWARE THAT YOUNG CHILDREN COULD SWALLOW SMALL PIECES.

OCR, JUNE 2003

3   A pictorial view of a house sign used by a firm of estate agents is shown below.
The sign is made from corrugated plastic (corriflute).
The outline shape is formed from two ellipses both with a major axis of 700mm and a
minor axis of 400mm.

(a) Draw accurately to a scale 1:5, an outline of a template which could be used when
cutting out the corrugated plastic signs.

(4 marks)

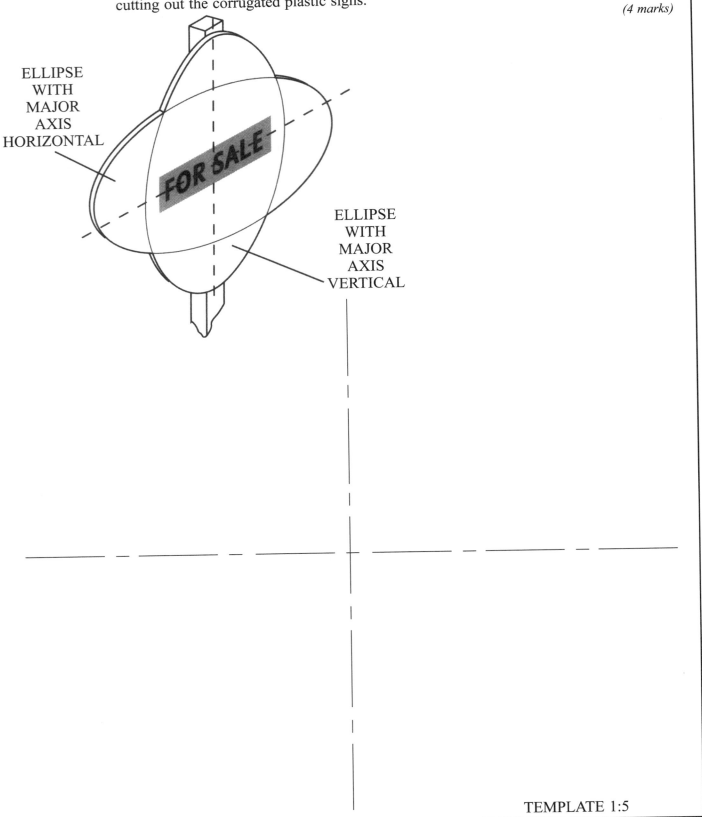

ELLIPSE
WITH
MAJOR
AXIS
HORIZONTAL

ELLIPSE
WITH
MAJOR
AXIS
VERTICAL

TEMPLATE 1:5

(b) Identify **one** problem when cutting out shapes from corrugated plastic.

....

(1 mark)

(c) Give **one** reason why the use of thermochromic inks might help to promote public interest in the house signs.

....

(1 mark)

(d) Use sketches and notes to show a simple method of changing the front of the house sign from **FOR SALE** to **SOLD**.
Include details of components and materials in your design.

(3 marks)

(e) Give **one** reason why corrugated plastic would be considered a safe material to use for the house sign.

....

(1 mark)

OCR, JUNE 2004

4   A design for an item of novelty packaging, made from thin card, is shown below.

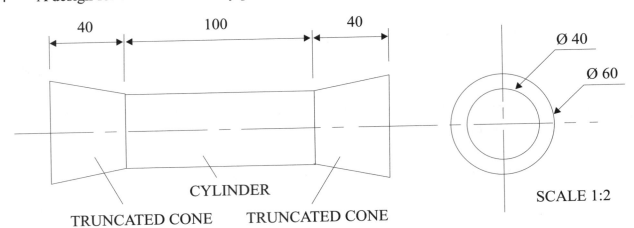

(a) A prototype has been made from three separate developments (nets).
     Use an exploded sketch to show a method of joining the cylinder to one of the
     truncated cones.

(2 marks)

(b) Draw an accurate full size drawing of the development (net) of **one** of the truncated cones.

(6 marks)

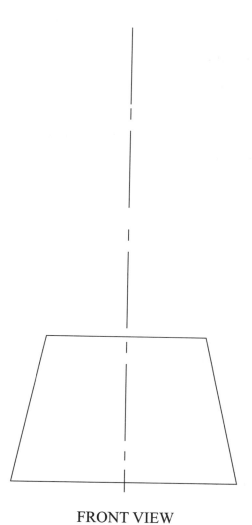

FRONT VIEW
OF CONE SECTION

(c) Quality checks have shown gaps where the cylinder and the truncated cone join together. Give **two** reasons for these gaps.

(2 marks)

OCR, JUNE 2004

5   **This question is about mechanisms.**

A promotional product made from card is shown below.
When the tab is pulled the puppy's ears move.

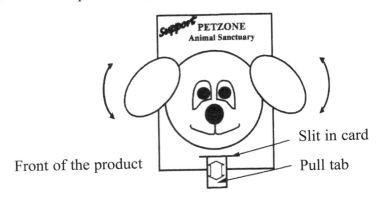

Front of the product

Slit in card

Pull tab

(a) The back of the product, shown below, shows part of the linkage mechanism used to move the ears. Strips of card form the linkage.

On the diagram below, add the working mechanism and include: all card levers and sliders or slits necessary for the ears to move when the tab is pulled.

(6 marks)

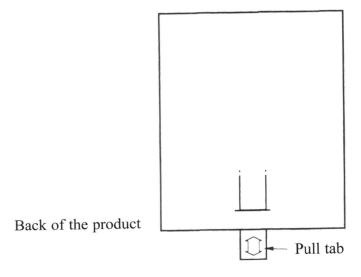

Back of the product

Pull tab

(b) Explain how the mechanism works.

....

....

....

....

....

....

(2 marks)

(c) (i) Use notes and sketches to show how you would join the card strips together to make a loose connection.

(3 marks)

(ii) Name any **two** components you have used.

....

(1 mark)

....

(1 mark)

AQA, JUNE 2003

126

6   **This question is about materials.**

(a) The air freshener (**Figure 1**) is in a 'blister' pack. It can be made by hand and rendered in school using the equipment shown below.

Complete the chart by:

(i)   naming each item of equipment shown;

(ii) explaining its use in the making of the backing card.

One example has been completed for you.

Figure 1

Equipment	Name	Use on the backing card
	Air brush	*To add background colour to the card.*
	....	....
	....	....
	....	....
	....	....

(8 marks)

Leave blank

(b) Materials have properties which make them suitable for different uses.

Study the list of materials below and give a different reason why each is suitable for the given use.

One example has been completed for you.

Materials	Typical Use	Reason
Vegetable Protein Board	Fast food box	*Made from vegetable material and is biodegradable*
Polystyrene sheet	'Blister' packs	
Foam core board	Architectural models	
Acrylic sheet	Shop signs	
Corrugated Board	Packaging	
Block Foam	Model buildings	

(5 marks)

(c) Smart materials have replaced more traditional materials. The forehead thermometer **(Figure 2)** is an alternative to a glass thermometer.

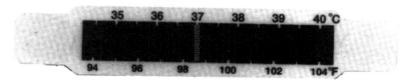

Reproduced by kind permission of The Boots Company PLC

Figure 2

Explain how a smart material is used in this type of thermometer.

....

....

....

....

....

....

(4 marks)

AQA, JUNE 2004

7   **This question is about Computer Aided Designing and Manufacturing and is worth 13 marks.**

backing card

The car air freshener shown **(Figure 3)** has a distinctive shaped backing card. It is important that all backing cards made are the same shape and size.

Three identical backing cards are to be cut from every A4 sheet of printed card.

Figure 3

(a) **Figure 4** shows the major CAD/CAM stages, in random order, involved in producing a batch of 30 identical backing cards.

(i) Re-arrange the given stages by writing the stage **number** or **letter** in the appropriate cell of the incomplete flow-chart **(Figure 5)**.

(7 marks)

(ii) Add **two** feedback loops for quality control.

(2 marks)

	STAGE	DESCRIPTION
CAD	*A*	*Load program*
	B	Copy and paste card outline twice
	C	Draw one backing card outline
	D	Is the design layout OK?

	1	STOP
CAM	2	Send design to cutter
	3	Have 30 cards been cut?
	4	Cut out the backing card

Figure 4

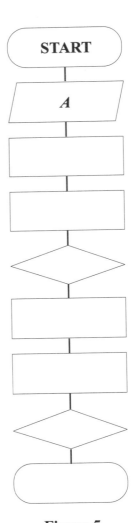

Figure 5

(b) (i) Explain **one** advantage of using CAD/CAM in batch production.

....

....

....

(2 marks)

(ii) Explain **one** disadvantage of using CAD/CAM in batch production.

....

....

....

(2 marks)

AQA, JUNE 2004

8   **This question is about environmental and social issues and is worth 26 marks.**

Figure 6 shows **three** different car air fresheners inside their packaging.

Figure 6

(a) Give **two** reasons why air fresheners are contained inside sealed packages.

Reason 1 ....

....

Reason 2 ....

....

(4 marks)

(b) (i) Are the transparent parts of the packages in **Figure 6** made from renewable or non-renewable material?

Explain your answer.

They are made from ....

materials because ....

....

(2 marks)

(ii) After opening, the packages in **Figure 6** are thrown away.

Explain the long term effect on the environment of the following materials if they are not correctly disposed of.

the backing card: ....

....

....

(3 marks)

the transparent materials: ....

....

....

(3 marks)

131

(c) In the box below draw and colour a symbol which shows that a package contains 50% recycled material.

(5 marks)

(d) Give **one** reasoned advantage and **one** reasoned disadvantage of using recycled paper and board.

(i) Advantage: ....

Reason: ....

....
(2 marks)

(ii) Disadvantage: ....

Reason: ....

....
(2 marks)

(e) (i) Explain why recycled paper should *not* be used for food packaging.

....

....

....
(2 marks)

(ii) Explain **one** unwanted effect on the local environment that is near to a "fast food" shop.

....

....
(2 marks)

(iii) How can a graphic designer of fast-food packaging encourage people to care about their local environment?

....
(1 mark)

AQA, JUNE 2004

Leave blank

Section One — The Design Process
Page 14 (Warm-up Questions)
1) The brief.
2) Possible answers: Questionnaire; survey; disassembly; search information sources like the Internet, books, magazines and adverts.
3) Possible answers: Shape; size; colour; cost; materials; appeal; texture; usability; construction or house style.
4) Design development is where you look at ways to change, improve, enhance, modify or adapt the initial design.
5) Tasks and time.
6) Decisions and quality control.

Page 15 (Exam Questions)
3   Because the brief is unclear, there could be confusion between Bruce and the phone company. If both of them don't have a shared understanding of the objectives there could be disagreement. Time and effort could be wasted on good designs which aren't suitable for the client's purposes.
(2 marks for answers that show problems for both the designer and client. 1 mark for answers that show problems for only one party.)

4 a) Do you prefer container shapes that are flat or upright? Which colour scheme do you like the most, a, b, c or d?
(2 marks for each closed question that relates to a relevant design attribute, which gives options for the answers. 1 mark for each closed question without options. 0 marks for open questions.)
In questionnaires you should normally ask closed questions — ones that have a definite answer or a limited number of answers, like 'Which do you prefer, red or green?'. It helps you get information you can analyse and use.

   b) i) To find out what people want the product to be like. *(1 mark)*
      ii) To make sure the product satisfies consumer requirements. *(1 mark)*
      iii) The criteria (standards) in the design specification are based on the survey results. *(2 marks)*

5 a) Because there might be lots of different creative ways to satisfy the brief. *(1 mark)*
   b) Possible answers: By producing detailed sketches; working out sizes/dimensions of components, features or the whole product; working out the precise position of components and features; asking for other people's opinions.
(3 marks available, 1 mark for each valid answer.)
Design development is any activity that moves rough ideas towards complete satisfaction of the brief.

6 a) Possible answers: • Test the model's volume;
   • test the strength of materials;
   • test components;
   • test stacking potential;
   • carry out market research into aesthetics;
   • test secondary packaging.
(3 marks available, 1 mark for each valid answer.)
   b) Possible answers: • He would have evidence to show if:
   • people liked the design;
   • its size/volume was correct;
   • the materials were suitable;
   • it compared well to existing products;
   • the products or its components worked properly.
(3 marks available, 1 mark for each valid answer showing useful evidence about market preferences.)

7 a) An answer along the lines of: It's a series of statements and drawings which show exactly how the product should be made. It gives precise instructions, dimensions and technical details.
(3 marks for detailed answers showing the strong link between

the manufacturer's specification and the exact construction details. 2 marks for showing some link between the specification and making. 1 mark for a limited understanding of the connection. 0 marks for no connection.)*
   b) Possible answers: • Machinery to be used; type of adhesive to use;
   • finishing processes;
   • exact product sizes/dimensions;
   • type of construction to use;
   • size and speed of machines;
   • tolerances.
(3 marks available, 1 mark for each valid answer.)

Section Two — Materials and Components
Page 28 (Warm-up Questions)
1) Layout paper.
2) Grams per square metre.
3) Thermoplastics.
4) Expanded polystyrene.
5) Injection moulding.
6) A material that changes in response to a stimulus.

Page 29 (Exam Questions)
3 a) Line bending (or strip bending). *(1 mark)*
   b) Blow moulding. *(1 mark)*
   c) Possible answers: • Thermochromatic ink;
   • lenticular plastic;
   • holographic effect embossed film;
   • phosphorent pigment;
   • chameleon card;
   • simulated metal card.
(2 marks available, 1 mark for each valid answer.)
There are lots of possible answers to this question, but it's only worth 2 marks, so you only need to give two answers.

4 a) Lamination (encapsulation) or varnishing.
(1 mark for either of the above terms.)
   b) Lamination: card is sandwiched between two layers of plastic, the sandwich is heated and bonds together.
Varnishing: varnish is sprayed onto the pre-printed card, the varnish dries as the solvent evaporates.
(2 marks for either complete method shown above. 1 mark for explaining some, but not the whole process.)

Page 39 (Warm-up Questions)
1) To explain a concept in 3D.
2) Blackness.
3) Directly with the pastel stick or with cotton wool.
4) French curves.
5) Resin and hardener.

Page 40 (Exam Questions)
3 a) Hot-wire cutter. *(1 mark)*
   b) Possible answers: Hot melt glue, superglue or double-sided tape.
(2 marks for any secure and appropriate fixing method.)
Hint: Think about the type of materials being glued. In this case balsa cement wouldn't be any good.
   c) Possible answers: Coping saw or reciprocating fret saw.
(2 marks for naming either saw. 1 mark for brand named machine e.g. Hegner.)
Questions about the right type of saw to use, so make sure you know which saws can be used for what.
   d) The waxed paper is positioned, and then the lettering is rubbed down.
(2 marks for giving both stages. 1 mark for only giving one stage.)

Page 55 (Warm-up Questions)
1) To explain a concept in 3-D.

2)   Complementary/contrasting.

3)   Italic.

Page 56 (Exam Questions)

4 a) 4 sheets. *(1 mark)*

   b) Cyan, magenta, yellow, key/black. *(1 mark for each correct colour.)*

   c) i) Small dots of each process colour are printed close together. *(1 mark for mentioning the colour of dots, 1 mark for mentioning the size of dots.)*

      ii) The dots of colour are too small and close together for the eye to see them individually, so this causes fusion of colour. *(1 mark for mentioning dot size, 1 mark for using 'fusion'.) The key idea here is that the dots are tiny which causes 'fusion of colour' to the naked eye.*

5 a) Possible answers: • To stay at the leading edge of industrial manufacturing methods;
   • to keep up with the competition;
   • to allow the equipment to work overnight on complex jobs;
   • to remove human boredom with repetitive work;
   • cost effective in the long run.
   (2 marks available, 1 mark for each valid answer.)

   b) Possible answers: It's much quicker, and effort can go into better design, rather than craft skill.
   (2 marks available, 1 mark for each valid answer.)

Page 68 (Warm-up Questions)

1)   Because they can make graphs more attractive, visually interesting, or easier to understand.

2)   Pictographs or pictograms.

3)   They give a visual clue about how to do something without words.

4)   Aircraft, airport or planes.

5)   Possible answers: • To show the order in which events have to be done to complete a task;
   • to provide a making guide;
   • to provide a method of quality control;
   • to identify where problems are occurring during the production process.

Page 69 (Exam Questions)

3 a)

(2 marks for any suitable logo using the letters PCZ.) If you're asked to design something make sure it's appropriate for the situation or company in the question.

   b) Possible answers: • Company vehicles;
   • company clothing;
   • company building - entrance/reception;
   • company products;
   • company stationery;
   • company literature;
   • company equipment;
   • company web site.
   (4 marks available, 1 mark for each valid answer.)

   c) They can be easily recognised without words and when they are reduced in size. It makes them easier to recognise when they're applied to different surfaces.
   (2 marks available, 1 mark for each valid answer.)

4 a) Possible answers: Draw it correctly on a computer and then use the Flip command. Or draw it inverted. *(2 marks)*

   b) Possible answers: Vinyl cutter or a plotter fitted with a cutter instead of a pen. *(2 marks)*

Page 79 (Warm-up Questions)

1)   It's morally good to care for the environment and its finite/non-sustainable resources. It's ethically good to consider future generations who could also use the oil we save by re-cycling plastics.

2)   British Standards Institute.

3)   Possible answers: • Name and address of the manufacturer;
   • cooking instructions;
   • ingredients;
   • country of origin;
   • preservatives and colourants;
   • storage instructions;
   • weight/volume;
   • additives;
   • best-before/use by date.

4)   Possible answers: Customer feedback helps manufacturers to:
   • improve the product;
   • make similar products with the same appeal;
   • find out why customers chose this product.

5)   To stop people making money from stealing other people's ideas from which they can make money.

Page 80 (Exam Questions)

3 a) Possible answers: • What kind of styling people prefer;
   • what fashionable trends make people buy new products;
   • what sort of advertising makes people buy this sort of product;
   • how much people are willing to spend on this type of product.
   (3 marks available, 1 mark for each valid answer.) There's nearly always an exam question about research so it's well worth learning all about it.

   b) Possible answers: • How much time is needed to set up new moulds and assembly line?
   • how much time is needed to manufacture parts and assemble together?
   • is manufacturing equipment for every stage of the work available?
   • are materials and components readily available?
   • can they make it look attractive and appealing to customers?
   • can they make it function as the customer wants?
   • are all of the criteria above cost effective?
   (3 marks available, 1 mark for each valid answer.)

4 a) Safety: Possible answers include: Is our factory safe?
   Are workers taking sick days because of the way we work?
   (1 mark for suitable safety question.)

   b) Ergonomics: Possible answers include: Can we find easier ways for workers to do the jobs that need doing?
   Are we friendly to people with disabilities?
   Are the workers bored?
   (1 mark for suitable question about ergonomics.)

   c) Environmental: Possible answers include: Do people like the work environment in the factory?
   What can we do to make the place more pleasant?
   (1 mark for suitable question about the work environment.)

Page 89 (Warm-up Questions)

1)   Using the internet or email attachments.

2)   Possible answers: For research purposes, to get expert knowledge or information about products.

3)   Possible answers: • Models can be viewed from any position;
   • compatibility of moving parts can be checked;
   • models can be re-sized and scaled;
   • virtual material stresses can be measured;
   • parts libraries can be utilized.

4)   Possible answers: • It can be used to show a product with more than one material/texture in realistic surfaces;
   • different colours can be given to different parts;
   • shading and light source are examples of refined rendering.
   All of these give the designer and the client a better appreciation

of the model.

5) Possible answers: • It allows the easy re-positioning of graphics and text, saving time and money;
• fonts can be re-sized on screen;
• scanned images can be imported into DTP;
• images can be sized and cropped in DTP;
• flexible and creative page layout is made straightforward.

Page 90 (Exam Questions)

4 a) It saves space. *(1 mark)*

b) Possible answers: Hard disks, CD, DVD, Zip, floppy disk. *(1 mark for each answer, up to a max. of 2 marks.)*

5 a) Possible answers: • No loose clothing, sleeves etc.;
• protect clothes by using an apron;
• tie back long hair;
• use protective equipment like goggles, face mask, breathing mask.
(1 mark for each of the above answers or other appropriate answers, up to a max. of 3 marks.)

b) Possible answers: Warning signs; ear protection; barriers; non-slip flooring; guards; dust/fume extraction.
(1 mark for each valid answer, up to a max. of 3 marks.)

6 Possible answers: • It can save time and reduce errors;
• it takes up less manufacturing space, which is expensive;
• it can operate with toxic gases given off by the materials it cuts, so there's no need for expensive safety equipment for workers;
• it can handle more complex jobs more accurately in less time;
• repeat jobs can be loaded from file and started on quickly.
(2 marks available, 1 mark for each valid answer.)
CAD and CAM play a big part in design and manufacturing, which makes it a favourite topic with the examiners — so make sure you know your stuff.

Page 106 (Warm-up Questions)

1) Input, process and output. Or input, transform and output.
2) Protection, preservation and promotion.
3) Cylindrical.
4) Water.
5) To position or align materials for drilling, sawing, etc.

Page 107 (Exam Questions)

2 a) To reduce costs. *(1 mark)*

b) Possible answers: • Customers associate quality packaging with quality merchandise;
• attractive packaging is appealing to customers;
• impression of better appearance than some competitors' products.
(1 mark for stating it suggests quality and 1 mark for commenting on increased customer appeal. Total of 2 marks.)

3 a) Linkage. *(1 mark)*

b) *(1 mark for correct shape linkage, 1 mark for both moving pivots drawn in correct place, 1 mark for fixed pivot drawn in correct place. Maximum 3 marks.)*

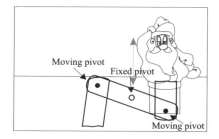

c) *(1 mark for correct labelling of fixed pivot, 1 mark for correct labelling of one or more moving pivots. Maximum 2 marks.)*
If you're asked to draw any diagrams in the exam make sure they are clear and labelled.

Practice Exam Paper

1 a) i)

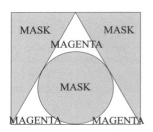

(2 marks for accurately drawn circle, not freehand. 1 mark for identifying 3 magenta areas.)

a) ii)

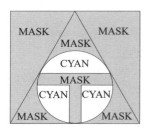

(1 mark for identifying the three cyan areas. 1 mark for drawing a circle that's consistent with your answer to part (i). 1 mark for drawing the letter T in the circle between 8-12mm wide.)

b) Cyan — blue or turquoise. *(1 mark. Green doesn't get any marks.)*
Magenta — red, pink or fuchsia. *(1 mark. Purple or salmon don't get any marks.)*

c) i) Possible answers: Use of the Internet to send designs and email;
video conferencing makes it easier to communicate their needs over large distances;
CD-ROMs can be used to send copies of the designs.
(1 mark for any one of these answers.)

ii) Possible answers: Improved ways to produce plates and colour separation;
invention of digital printing;
laser printers can be used to print things quickly.
(1 mark for any one of these answers.)

2 **Target age group** — Indicating an age range the product is suitable for *(1 mark)*. Mentioning how long it would hold interest for or whether it is difficult or easy to make *(1 mark)*.
Materials — Stating it should be made of thin card *(1 mark)*. Mentioning any of the following factors about it: ease, printing, cutting, folding, assembling or glueing the product *(1 mark)*.
Manufacture — Naming a commercial printing method, i.e. off-set litho, digital printing, flexography *(1 mark)*. Commenting on the artwork preparation or pre-creasing or die cutting *(1 mark)*.
Quality control — Considering quality control in relation to the printing, i.e. registration or print quality *(1 mark)*. Quality control issues relating to assembly, i.e. consistency of sizes of different pieces or edging matching up *(1 mark)*.
Health and safety — Mentioning that there should be a warning on the pack or no apparent risk *(1 mark)*. Hazards identified, i.e. sharp tools, toxic glue, swallowing pieces, or explaining why there are no hazards *(1 mark)*.
(Total of 10 marks.)

3 a) Applying the scale to both major and minor axes of the sketch *(1 mark)*. Completed drawing with good construction *(2 marks)*, good construction method partially completed *(1 mark)*. Template accurate representation of the original picture *(1 mark)*. *(Total of 4 marks.)*

b) It's more difficult to cut in one direction than the other because of the corrugations. *(1 mark. Other answers are possible.)*

c) Different temperatures could be used to change the colour of the design on the sign. *(1 mark, no marks if you don't mention BOTH colour and temperature.)*

d) Identifying a suitable method, i.e. separate piece of plastic to put over FOR SALE *(1 mark)*. Stating the method of attachment *(1 mark, but no marks for screws, nails, sellotape or glue)*. Giving details of appropriate materials, i.e. waterproof and graphic products *(1 mark)*.

e) Possible answers: It bends easily if walked into; no damage is caused if it's blown away from the stake. *(1 mark for either answer.)*

4 a)

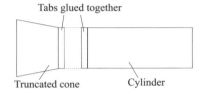

Tabs glued together

Truncated cone   Cylinder

Exploded sketch in 2D or 3D, inline *(1 mark)*. Using a suitable method, i.e. tabs *(1 mark)*. *(Total of 2 marks.)*

b) Identifying the apex of the truncated cone *(1 mark)*. Showing the base arc struck from the apex *(1 mark)*. Splitting the base diameter into 6 or 12 *(1 mark)*. Drawing 12 divisions set off round the base arc *(1 mark)*. Drawing all the development's measurements to full size and within the tolerance *(1 mark)*. Drawing the second curve *(1 mark)*. *(Total of 6 marks.)*
The apex is the top of the cone.

c) Possible answers: • The circumferences aren't accurate enough;
• it's hard to join the tabs;
• glue and parts often slip when drying;
• the tabs are too wide.
(1 mark for each reason, up to 2 marks.)

5 a)

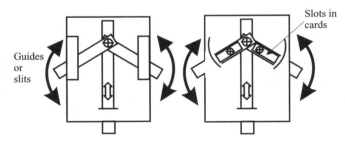

Slots in cards

Guides or slits

Putting guides, slits and pivots in roughly the right place *(1 mark for each)*. Continuing the pull tab within the rectangle *(1 mark)*. Drawing the arms in proportion to the pull tab *(1 mark)*. If it would work in practice *(1 mark)*. *(Total of 6 marks.)*

b) Good explanation of moving parts and how they relate to your design *(2 marks)*. Some explanation of how the moving parts relate to your design, but with some details missed out *(1 mark)*. *(Total of 2 marks.)*

c)

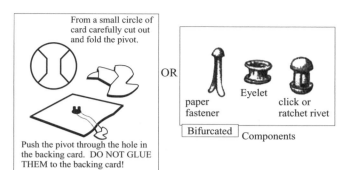

From a small circle of card carefully cut out and fold the pivot.

OR

paper fastener   Eyelet   click or ratchet rivet

Bifurcated   Components

Push the pivot through the hole in the backing card. DO NOT GLUE THEM to the backing card!

Paper pivot

i) Clear sketches and notes showing the card and fastener and how it's aligned and assembled, including the hole *(3 marks)*. Sketches and notes that are correct, but missing a couple of details *(2 marks)*. Sketches and notes that aren't very clear or that are missing lots of details *(1 mark)*. Using glue *(0 marks)*.

ii) Possible answers: Split pin; butterfly pin; brass fastener; star binders, paper fasteners; crimped eyelet.
(2 marks for correctly naming the component(s) in the list above in your sketch. 1 mark for identifying the name of the component(s) in your sketch but that aren't in the list.)

6 a) i) Names of equipment: Stencil;
spirit, Pantone, felt tip pen, or marker pen;
craft knife, modelling knife, or balsa knife;
hot glue gun, glue gun, or low melt glue.
(1 mark for each correctly identified piece of equipment, up to 4 marks.)

ii) Uses of the equipment: Lettering; adding outline or details; cutting modelling materials;
gluing 'blister' to card, giving shape to the card.
(1 mark for each correct use, up to 4 marks.)

b) Polystyrene sheet — as a thermoplastic it's mouldable. *(1 mark)*
Foam core board (foamboard) — it's a flat, good surface that's easily worked. *(1 mark)*
Acrylic — it's translucent. *(1 mark)*
Corrugated board — it's energy absorbent and easily worked. *(1 mark)*
Block foam — it takes finishes and is lightweight. *(1 mark)*

c) Heat causes the crystals in the film to change colour, seen on the outside by temperature marker. When the crystals are cool they change back to black and the temperature bar disappears. The process is reversible.
(4 marks for a clear and accurate description. 3 marks for some understanding of the general principles, referring to inks, crystals etc.
2 marks for an understanding and using basic terms, mentioning colour and temperature. 1 mark for vague answer describing how a thermometer works.)

136

7 a)

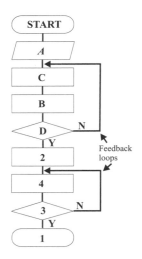

i) *(1 mark for each correct position in flow chart. Total of 7 marks.)*

ii) *(1 mark for each correctly positioned feedback loop. Total of 2 marks.)*

b) i) Possible answers: it helps to ensure uniformity of a design; it speeds up the whole process; it makes it a lot easier to make changes.
(2 marks for a good justified answer. 1 mark for a one word answer.)

ii) Possible answers: the equipment can be really expensive; staff have to be trained to use it, which costs time and money; there is the risk of errors in production.
(2 marks for a good justified answer. 1 mark for a one word answer.)

8 a) Possible answers: To protect the air freshener; to preserve the smell; to avoid any contamination; to make it tamper proof; to provide information about the product or company.
(2 marks for each correct reason. 1 mark for a correct reason that's a one word answer.)

b) i) Non-renewable materials *(1 mark)*, *because* they are plastic, which is an oil based material, and oil is a finite resource *(1 mark)*.

ii) Backing card — Possible answer: It creates unsightly litter. But it's made from bio-degradable material so it will eventually rot away.
(3 marks for a well explained answer that clearly shows how the backing card could effect the environment e.g. stating that it's bio-degradable so will rot away. 2 marks for an answer that's not fully explained. 1 mark for a correct but unexplained answer, e.g. it causes litter.)
The transparent materials — Possible answer: It creates unsightly litter which isn't bio-degradable, so it won't ever decompose. Small animals could eat it and become sick or die.
(3 marks for a well explained answer that clearly shows how the backing card could effect the environment e.g. stating that it's not bio-degradable so it won't decompose. 2 marks for an answer that's not fully explained. 1 mark for a correct but unexplained answer, e.g. it causes litter.)

c)

(1 mark for stating 50%. 1 mark for colouring it green or black. 3 marks for drawing either symbol accurately, making the arrow(s) wide and the shape round. 2 marks if the symbol is almost right but is missing some detail. 1 mark for making some connection to the correct symbol. Total of 5 marks.)

d) i) Possible answers: it's more environmentally friendly as it means less litter is created; it helps to preserve resources because it uses already existing material instead of being made from new trees.
(1 mark for stating an advantage, and 1 mark for explaining it.)

ii) Possible answers: recycled paper and board is poorer quality than non-recycled paper and board, so printing ink is more likely to bleed; recycled paper and board is a beige colour which can make it look less attractive.
(1 mark for giving a disadvantage, and 1 mark for explaining it.)

e) i) There is a greater risk of the food being contaminated by germs or toxic substances which the paper has been exposed to during the recycling process. Contamination might make the customer sick, and they wouldn't buy the product again.
(1 mark for mentioning contamination by germs or toxic substances. 1 mark for explaining where the source of contamination comes from or the consequences for the customer.)

ii) Possible answers: customers may spill food on floor; increased litter due to people throwing wrappers on the floor instead of the bin; increased risk of vermin due to extra bins and discarded food.
(1 mark for stating a problem, 1 mark for explaining how the fast food restaurant would actually cause the problem.)

iii) Possible answers: include messages on packaging about putting litter in bins; design a poster or advertising campaign about it; design signs that can be displayed in or outside the restaurant; put messages or logos about recycling on the packaging.
(1 mark)

Working out your Grade

- Find your average percentage for the whole exam.
- Look it up in this table to see what grade you got. If you're borderline, don't push yourself up a grade — the real examiners won't.

Average %	85+	74 – 84	61 – 73	47 – 60	37 – 46	29 – 36	22 – 28	15 – 21	under 15
Grade	A*	A	B	C	D	E	F	G	U

Important
- This is a Higher paper — if you're doing Foundation, you'll need more marks in the real exam.
- Obviously these grades are only a guide, and the more practice you do the better...

THE ANSWERS

Index

Symbols

2-D design software 62
2-D pattern 62
2-D views 60
2-point perspective 44
3-D 42, 44, 46
3-D bar charts 63
3-D objects 60, 62
3-D sketches 44
3rd angle orthographic projection 60

A

A4 paper 18, 50
accentuating shapes 46
accurate drawings 44
acetate 20
acrylic 20
acrylic cement 34
active materials 24
actual size 61
adaptive materials 24
additive colours 49
adequate ventilation 88
adhesives 34
Adobe Illustrator 38
Adobe PageMaker 38, 84
Adobe Photoshop 31, 38, 85
advertising 42, 66, 71
aerosol adhesives 34
aesthetics 8
airbrushes 31
all-body suits 88
angles 32
annotate 9
antioxidants 26
Araldite 34
Art Roc 27
assembly drawings 61
automatic base 62
axonometric projections 32

B

backgrounds 30
balsa cement 34
bar charts 63
barcodes 105
batch production 96
beam compasses 33
biodegradable 74
biological materials 26
blister packs 21
blow moulding 22, 98
blu-tack 34
board 19
booklets 51
bow compasses 33
boxes 62
brainstorm 8
brand loyalty 71
branding 66
briefs 5, 109
British Electrotechnical Approvals Board (BEAB) 77
British Standards Institute (BSI) 77
British Standards Kitemark 77
British Toy and Hobby Manufacturers' Association 77

C

CAD (see computer-aided design)
CAD software 45, 48
CAM (see computer-aided manufacture)
CAM machine 104
cams 94

car-body filler 27
carbon fibre 26
cardboard mounts 51
cartoons 58
cartridge paper 18
casting 88
cell production 97
chalk pastel 30
charts 63, 64
child labour 74
clamping 88
clipart 85
CMY (cyan, magenta and yellow) 49
CMYK (cyan, magenta, yellow and black) 49, 85
colour 48, 49, 54
colour density 98
colour registration marks 98
colour wheel 48
coloured pencils 47
commercial products 98
compass cutters 35
compasses 33
complementary colours 48
composite materials 99
computer images 105
computer numerically controlled (CNC) 83
computer-aided design (CAD) 81, 104, 62
computer-aided manufacture (CAM) 62, 82, 104, 97
consumer 71, 77
container 62
continuous data 64
continuous production 96
control and feedback 92, 93
coping saw 35, 36
Corel Photo-Paint 85
CorelDraw 38
corporate identity 66
corriflute 21, 37, 101
corrugated card 19
corrugated plastic 21, 37
COSHH 77
cost 71, 73
costings 12
cow gum 19
craft knives 35
crating 44
creasing 102
creasing bars 35, 102
crop marks 98
cube 44, 62
curves 33
customer 42, 52
customer research 5
cutting 102
cutting tools 35, 102
cylinder 62

D

David's Isopon 27
deburring metal 88
decision box 93
depth 46
design brief 5
design process 5
design specification 7
designers 42
desk top publishing (DTP) 38, 84
details 42, 52
development 10
die cutting 35, 98, 102
digital camera 54, 85
disassembly 6
disposal of waste 74, 75, 88

dot shading 46
dot-matrix printers 46
dowelling 36
down time 96
drawing boards 32
drawing media 30, 31
drawing pins 37
drill bits 36
drilling machines 83, 88
driving licences 53
dry printing process 38
dry transfer lettering 30
DTP (see Desk Top Publishing)
dumb materials 24
duplex board 19
dust 88
dust extraction equipment 88

E

e-mail 86
electricity 24
electro-luminescent panels 24
Electronic Data Interchange (EDI) 86
embossed 98
embossing 102
emergency 88
encapsulation 27, 53
enhancement 46, 47, 48, 49
environmental issues 75, 76
environmental responsibility 74
environmentally friendly 19, 34
epoxy resin glue 34
eraser guides 33
ergonomics 73
evaluate 10
evaluation 11, 72, 73, 112, 113
exploded drawings 61
extrusion 22
eye level 59
eyelets 37

F

face visors 88
fading 51
fashion 42, 71
feedback 93
felt-tipped pens 18, 31
files 36
fillers 27
finishes 54
finishing 27
fixative spray 51
fixings 37
flame cutters 83
flammable liquids 88
flash 99
flexicurves 33
flexography 98, 100
flow charts 13, 67, 93
foamboard 19
focus groups 73
foil application 102
foil blocking 102
follower (cams) 94
forces 95
formative evaluation 11
formers 104
frame 51
frame based software 84
freehand sketching 9, 43
French curves 33
fret saw 35
fulcrum 94
function of a product 73

Index

Index

Let's face it, you want _CGP_ Revision Books — not other people's dreary stuff.

Everyone else just gives you dreary revision books with only the boring stuff in and no entertainment. Boo. Hiss. We're different — we always try and make sure you're gonna enjoy using our books.

What you _really_ need is a _**Free Catalogue**_ showing the full range of CGP Revision Books. That way you can be sure you're not missing out on a brilliant book that _**might just save your life**_.

At CGP we **work our socks off** to despatch your stuff really quickly.
If you get your order to us before 5.00pm (Mon-Fri) you should get it next day — most of the time, anyway.

(Obviously, if you order on Saturday night on a bank holiday weekend then you won't get it 'til Wednesday morning at the very earliest — no matter how hard we try!)

FIVE ways to get your Free Catalogue really quickly

- Phone: 0870 750 1252   (Mon-Fri, 8.30am to 5.30pm)
- Fax: 0870 750 1292
- E-mail: orders@cgpbooks.co.uk
- Post: CGP, Kirkby in Furness, Cumbria, LA17 7WZ
- Website: www.cgpbooks.co.uk

CGP books — available in all the best bookshops